Alok Ranjan

Population
and
Development

The Indian Perspective

Shyam Institute

Population and Development

The Indian Perspective

Alok Ranjan
Director

'Shyam' Institute of Public Cooperation
and Community Development
Datia, MP-475 661,
India

ISBN: 1-58112-844-4

First edition
Published in 1999

Published by
Universal Publishers/uPUBLISH.com
USA
1999

www.upublish.com/books/alok.htm

To

Amma and Daddy

Preface

The present monograph attempts to analyse experiences and concerns related to population and development in India through an empirical perspective. It is primarily concerned with establishing linkages between population growth trends and patterns with the social and economic development processes in the country. India, it may be pointed out, was the first country in the developing world to recognize the role of population factors in the process of social and economic development and to adopt a comprehensive population policy as a part of its social and economic development plan as early as in 1950. An analysis of Indian experience, therefore, may provide valuable insight about population and development interrelationship and can contribute toward integrating population factors in the social and economic development planning process. In this context, the present volume may be useful for development planners and development policy makers who are interested in giving a development orientation to population related issues.

Papers of this monograph are based on the assignments submitted for the award of Post Graduate Diploma in Population and Development of Jawaharlal Nehru University, New Delhi under the Global Programme of Training in Population and Sustainable Development of the United Nations Population Fund. They cover the core issues of the training programme in population and development including capital formation and savings, technology evolution, food supply, commercial energy use, environment, population policy, population transition, reproductive mortality, status of women and urbanization. Most of the papers included here are based on the empirical data and demonstrate the use of various analytical techniques and methods for the analysis of empirical observations and making interpretations. They can serve as reading material for any population and development training and research programme.

I am grateful to my advisors at the Centre for Development Studies, Trivandrum who reviewed the earlier draft of some of the papers included in this volume and gave important suggestions for improvement. I am also grateful to the 'Shyam' Institute for providing me necessary infrastructure and facilities for completing this work. Last but not least, I am grateful to my wife Sudha for providing me moral and family support for taking up this task.

Contents

Introduction

The question of life and death has been of paramount importance throughout the human history. In the prehistorical past, the limited technological capacity of the man had made the survival a difficult proposition. Life, at that time, was insecure and mortality rates were very high. Survival of the man, during these prehistoric days, was the greatest challenge to the mankind.

The quest for survival and a secure life made the man innovative and enterprising. Through sheer and sustained efforts which lasted for centuries, the man has now been able to win over a number of diseases and natural calamities that endangered the life in the past. The life, on the planet Earth, today, is more secure than it was in the past.

Population and Development: The Indian Perspective

The improved survival of the man, however, has resulted in a rapid increase in the number of human beings on Earth. This rapid population increase led some people to believe that, unlimited population growth, will eventually nullify the benefits of technological innovations and development that have ensured the security of life on Earth in the past. Initially, rapid population growth was alleged to causing underdevelopment and impoverishment of the masses. Subsequently, increased knowledge of environment and increased awareness of the environmental issues led to the claim that rapid population growth could ruin the environment and the natural resource base which are crucial for sustaining life on the Planet Earth. Rapid population growth was thus claimed to be endangering the very basis of the life on Earth. Since, most of this rapid population growth was confined to countries of Africa, Asia and Latin America which were comparatively poor to countries in North America and Europe in social and economic terms, it was also claimed that underdevelopment and poverty faced by these countries was basically the result of rapid population growth. Among such claims, and with confidence outrunning the data, a simple family planning model was forced upon the countries of the third World. It was argued that curtailing population growth rates as the result of the application of the simple family planning model would effectively address the problems of under development and rampant poverty. Family planning, in this argument, was viewed as a panacea to all development ills of the poor countries of the World.

The experience with the application of the simple family planning model, however, turned out to be a frustrating experience in most of the countries of Africa, Asia and Latin

America. Application of the model did result in the increase in the number of acceptors of family planning methods and associated decline in fertility levels which led to a slowdown in population growth rates in many countries but this slowdown in population growth rates could not be followed up by parallel improvements in the levels of income and associated improvements in living conditions and reduction of poverty. The much professed negative impact of rapid population growth on social and economic development was in question and so was the relevance of the simple family planning model in addressing the development ills of the poor. Contrary to the prevalent wisdom at that time, it was argued that an effective addressing of the problems of underdevelopment and poverty might also address the problem of rapid population growth in a more subtle manner. Family planning, in this alternative thinking, was not the most appropriate development strategy. Rather, it was stressed that development was the best contraceptive. In any case, the linkages between population factors and development concerns became the subject of intense discussion, debate and scientific enquiry.

At the same time and despite decrease in fertility levels and slowdown in population growth rates, the population of the World continued to increase largely due to the momentum generated by the high fertility in the immediate past. It is estimated that despite reduction in fertility levels and slowdown of population growth rates, the population of the World will stabilize somewhere around 10 billion by the middle of the next century. This increase in the population of the World has thrown a new challenge to the mankind - how to build a sustainable World that can ensure security of the life on the Planet Earth for future generations.

Population and Development: The Indian Perspective

Two key issues emerge from the foregoing discussions. First, there have been close, explicit or implicit, linkages between population factors and development issues throughout the human history. Second, the relationship between population factors and development concerns has been dynamic in nature on the scales of time and place. A given set of population and development concerns, when addressed, have been found to give way to another set of population and development related issues. On the other hand, the characterization of population and development relationship in one social cultural and environmental settings has been found to be out of context in other areas.

Given the transient nature of population and development relationship, it is clear that this relationship cannot be analysed and understood through a normative, theoretical approach. In fact, there is no well defined and unified theory for studying the linkages between population factors and development concerns. Since the relationship between population factors and development concerns vary substantially according to institutional structure of the economy and the society as well as according to the level of social and economic development, there is little point or usefulness in trying to develop a universal framework for analysing relationship between population factors and development issues. Development of such a framework is neither feasible nor desirable. Rather, the population and development interrelationship can best be discussed and understood through a context specific characterization approach. This approach is basically illustrative in nature and is built upon the empirical evidence that is available.

The present monograph employs the characterization approach to analysing and understanding population and development relationship and its consequences under specific social, environmental and cultural contexts. It is a collection of papers each of which is related to a specific human concern which has both population dimension as well as development dimension. This concern has been characterized on the basis of available empirical evidence and application of appropriate analytical tools. As such, the papers included in this monograph not only illustrate the nature of population and development relationship under different social, environmental and cultural contexts, they also provide frameworks for similar analyses under different settings using a different set of empirical evidence. In this way, the present monograph also serves as a reference manual for teaching, training and research activities that are focussed toward the linkages between population factors and development concerns.

The monograph consists of eleven papers in addition to this introduction. The first paper of the monograph analyses linkages between capital formation, savings and population growth on the basis of the time series data from India for the period 1957 through 1996. Findings of the analyses are then discussed in the light of prevailing theories and concepts that link population growth and economic development.

The second paper of the monograph is focussed towards an analysis of the past trends in the demand and supply of food in India and their future prospects. The paper concludes that substantial investment in the agriculture production systems of the country is required in order to meet out the demand of food in the country that will result from the increase in the population in future.

The linkage between population growth and technology evolution is the subject matter of the third paper of the monograph. The paper discusses, at length, how, in the past, population pressure and population growth might have played a key role in technology evolution and argues that, at present, technology evolution and technology development is guided more by capital gains.

An analysis of the trends and patterns in commercial energy use in 118 countries of the World during the period 1980 through 1994 is the subject matter of the fourth paper of the monograph. Analysis of the use of commercial energy is important in the context of environmental concerns as the wastes generated through the use of commercial energy are the key contributors to the environmental problems that the World is facing today.

The fifth paper of the monograph analyses, critically, the role of population and consumption in the context of environmental issues and concerns that the World is facing today. Using the empirical data on population growth and increase in commercial energy consumption, between 1965 and 1985, it is observed that the role of increase in per capita consumption is significantly more in important as compared to the role of population and its growth as far as the problems related to the environment are concerned.

The next two papers of the monograph are related to the population of India, the second most populous country of the World. India was also the first country in the World to adopt a well-defined population policy and to launch an official programme of population control as early as in 1952. The first of the two papers gives a narrative summary of the emergence and transition in population policy in India. It highlights the missed opportunities in the quest for addressing the problem of rapid population growth in the country. The second paper, on the other hand, analyses the past and future transition in the population of the country in greater detail by using a methodology that separates the level effects of fertility and mortality from their age structure effects. The analysis suggests that the momentum of the past population growth will lead to a slowdown in population transition in the country in the near future.

A comparison of fertility transition between China and India is the focus of attention of the next paper of the monograph. In the past, the demographic situation in the two countries was very similar. However, China has recently been able to reduce fertility and cut population growth rate very substantially whereas population growth in India still hovers around 2.0 per cent per year largely because of persistent high fertility. Using a decomposition methodology, this paper identifies salient features of success of population control efforts in China and reasons behind limited success of these efforts in India.

Ninth and tenth papers of the monograph are focussed on women. After the Cairo Conference on Population and Development, women's concerns have found an important place in the fields of population and development in the form of a reproductive health approach to addressing population problems and in the form of equality of women with men in the context of social and economic progress. In line with the above developments, the first of the two papers investigates the female reproductive age mortality in India through a parametric approach while the second paper analyses variations in the status of women across the States of the country. The analysis suggested that increase in income levels and associated infrastructure development may not ensure equality between men and women in a country like India particularly when the increase in income is oriented toward capital investment and concentration of services rather then investments in human beings and diffusion of technology.

The last paper of the monograph discusses the pattern of urbanization in India with particular emphasis on the growth of its largest city - Greater Bombay. It is widely argued that the rapid urbanization that the World is witnessing today is primarily due to a typical development approach that encourages rural to urban migration. The paper highlights the fact that little attention has been paid to social aspects of social and economic change in a country which is the pioneer of population policy and which has been engaged in farsighted economic planning since Independence.

The selection of the topics covered in the monograph is primarily based on the post graduate training course on population and development that has been sponsored by the United Nations Population Fund under its Global Programme of Training in Population and Sustainable Development. They are, obviously, not exhaustive in nature. Still they provide useful frameworks which may constitute the basis for analysing population and development relationships.

Capital Formation, Savings and Population Growth in India, 1957-96
An Empirical Investigation

Introduction

Attempts to link the size and growth of population with the levels of living are not of recent origin. Frequently, in the past, researchers have made attempts to explain how population growth and size determined income level which has been taken as a proxy for levels of living in the development research. One may mention here some extensive studies of Ricardo and Malthus in the 18th century which suggested that population growth beyond a limit was a major obstacle in improving standards of living of the majority of human race. In fact the law of diminishing returns propounded by Malthus led to the conviction that, sooner or later, human population will outgrow the subsistence required for its survival and so, ultimately, there will be misery and vice throughout the World (Malthus, 1798).

Conclusions derived by Malthus have been a subject of bitter criticism from many angles since the days of Malthus. This

9

criticism, in any case, has kept Malthusian perspective about population and its impact on social and economic development alive till today. In addition to this criticism, there have been events in the history of mankind which have repeatedly given a fresh lease of life to the debate on the impact of population and population related factors on the process of social and economic development.

Initial reaction to Malthusian conjecture was that of disbelief, and the intelligentia, particularly in Europe, tended to ignore it. The industrial revolution that occurred in Europe immediately after Malthus was the main evidence to ignore Malthusian perspective. There were unmistakable signs that subsistence levels could be increased to meet the needs of increased population through technological innovations.

Recently Boserup (1981) has put up the theory that population growth, in the 18th century England, was basically the motivating force behind technological innovations that led to the industrial revolution. In any case, Malthus remained practically ignored for more than two centuries. It was during the 1950s that Malthus surfaced again on the World development scenario in the neoclassical form. Some very substantial changes in the World political order were primarily responsible for the re-emergence of Malthus in the form of neo-Malthusian perspective. The Second World War was over and many countries of Asia, Africa and Latin America got freedom from colonial rule of European countries. Centuries of colonial rule had destroyed the economic structure of these countries and basically, there were no development efforts. The freedom that these countries got from the colonial rule was associated with abject poverty, unproductive agriculture, no

10

industrialisation and very little human resources development. Many of these countries had plenty of natural resources but did not have the technical knowledge necessary to tap these resources for their own betterment. In an attempt to improve levels of living, these countries had to start from somewhere and most of them logically opted to prevent untimely death from diseases and natural calamities. This focus, however, aggravated problems further as the decrease in death rates resulted in a rapid growth of population which the frail economy of many of these countries was not able to support and, instead of improving, the living standards actually deteriorated.

Thus among the rampant uncertainties of 1960s about how to promote development in the developing countries, the concept of reduction in population growth through birth control was mooted by the developed countries instead of sharing knowledge and technology. The study by Coale and Hoover (1958) on population growth and economic development in low income countries provided empirical and conceptual support to the idea.

But efforts to control birth rates through family planning programmes in developing countries met with stiff resistance from the society of these countries. There were serious reservations about the rationality of simple family planning model, and despite huge investments, family planning programmes could not succeed. Though official policies continue to insist upon increased efforts on population control, yet it is still not clear whether population control will lead to development or development will lead to a reduction in population growth rates. A number of studies carried out in the

1960s - Coale and Hoover (1958), Enke (1971) - have tried to impress upon that population control may lead to development at a faster pace. It may be interesting to analyse here how far the interpretations of these studies have withstood the empirical evidence collected since 1960s in a country like India.

The present paper attempts to analyse the relationship between capital formation, savings and population growth in India during the period between 1957-96. This period has been a period of turbulence in India. In this period, the country had three wars - with China and Pakistan. During this period there were three droughts which affected the economy significantly. It was in this period that economy was in a very poor shape. It was in this period that the population of the country provided a near ideal set up for verifying, empirically, the interpretations made by western economists and demographers on economic development and population growth in India.

Capital Formation
During the period 1950-51 to 1995-96, the net domestic capital formation in India, at 1980-81 prices, increased from Rs 45.01 billion to Rs 830.27 billion - an increase of Rs 785.26 billion. This amounts to, on average, an increase of nearly Rs 1.8 billion per year. This increase, however, was not uniform. The average annual exponential growth rate of net domestic capital formation at fixed prices varied between a high of 32.6 per cent in 1955-56 to a low of -38.8 per cent in 1952-53. Other years when net domestic capital formation recorded a negative growth were 1957-58, 1958-59, 1961-62, 1967-68, 1968-69, 1972-73, 1974-75, 1979-80, 1982-83, 1986-87, and 1991-92. In 1961-62, the country was at war with China whereas the slump in capital formation during 1967-69 and in 1972-73 may

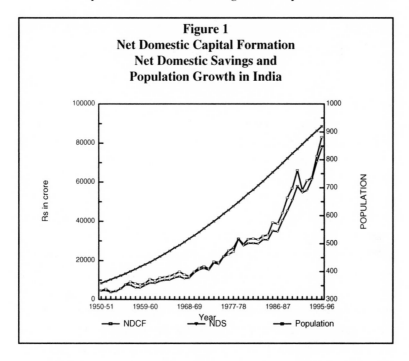

Figure 1
Net Domestic Capital Formation
Net Domestic Savings and
Population Growth in India

be attributed to the war with Pakistan, in 1965 and again in 1971. On the other hand, the decline in the capital formation in 1974-75, 1979-80, 1982-83, 1986-87 and 1991-92 may be attributed to internal disturbances in the country. The political instability during 1974-75 led to the clamping of the emergency; during 1979-80, there was political instability due to uncertain future of the Janata government; in1982-83, the Punjab problem was at its extreme while in 1986-87, the political environment of the country was charged with the Bofors issue. Lastly, during 1991-92, again there was a lot of political uncertainty about the future of the government in power. Thus, deviation from the path of a continuous increase in net capital domestic formation has been affected by more by exogenous variables such as war and political instability then by endogenous factors related to economy.

Savings
In 1950-51, net domestic savings at current prices accounted for 10.4 per cent of the gross domestic product of the country. This proportion increased to 25.6 per cent in the year 1995-96. Thus, over a period of 46 years since 1950-51, the savings rate in the country increased by 15.2 absolute per cent points. In terms of net amount, net domestic savings in the country increased from Rs 46 billion in 1950-51 to Rs 775.76 billion at 1980-81 prices - an increase of Rs 729.76 billion over a period of 46 years or an average annual increase of 1.7 billion per year.

It may be seen from table 1 that growth of net domestic savings has largely been responsible for the increase in net domestic capital formation in the country during the 45 years between 1950-51 and 1995-96. The simple zero order correlation coefficient between net domestic capital formation and net domestic savings at fixed prices has been estimated to be 0.85 which is statistically highly significant. Clearly, domestic savings have been the major contributor to net domestic capital formation in the country.

It may also be seen from the table that, barring a few exceptions, net domestic capital formation has always been more than the net domestic savings in the country. Out of the 46 years under reference, in only six years: 1950-51, 1952-54 and 1975-78 - the net domestic savings were more than the net domestic capital formation. The reason behind net domestic capital formation exceeding the net domestic savings is that external assistance and loans and borrowing have frequently been used for capital formation in addition to the resources that were available through net domestic savings.

Population Growth

Contrary to total net domestic capital formation and net domestic savings, population of the country increased uniformly throughout the period. This increase in population has been rated as rapid by international standards. The population of the country in 1950-51 was estimated to be around 359 million which increased to 920 million in 1995-96, an increase of about 561 million. This implies that, on average, population of the country increased at an average annual rate of growth of almost 2.1 per cent per year. According to the data provided by the Registrar General of India on the basis of decennial population censuses, the population of the country increased by 21.52 per cent during the decade 1951-61; by 24.57 per cent during 1961-71; by 24.98 per cent during 1971-81; and by 23.50 per cent during the decade 1981-91. Thus, in the 40 years between 1950 and 1991, the population of the country increased by more than 2.5 times the population in 1951.

During the same period, family planning was promoted and pursued at the official level to curtail the rapid growth of population. India was the first country in the World to adopt a well-defined population policy and an official programme of birth limitation as early as in 1952. The evidence of family planning activities in India is available from 1965 onwards in the form of family planning programme service statistics. These statistics show a continuous increase in the number of acceptors of various methods of fertility control that have been promoted under the programme (Government of India, 1996). But despite this increase in the number of acceptors of family planning in the country, there appeared little change in population growth during the period under reference. The population, during this period, increased continuously and rapidly.

Relationship between Capital Formation, Savings and Population Growth

What is the relationship between capital formation savings and population growth in India during 1950 through 1996? To answer this question, we have utilised the data given in table 1 to work out a model bringing out the essential linkage between net domestic capital formation, net domestic savings and population. The analysis that follows assumes that the capital formation in any economy is influenced by the level of investment which, in turn, is influenced by the savings and the growth in population.

To investigate the impact of net domestic savings and population growth on the net domestic capital formation in the country, we have applied the famous Cobb-Douglas Production function to the data on savings, domestic capital formation and population growth in India. The necessary information for different years is given in table 1. The Cobb-Douglas function is widely used to analyse the impact of labour input and capital input on the output. Here, we measure capital input in terms of net domestic savings and labour input in terms of the size of the population.

The Cobb-Douglas function, in its stochastic form, may be defined as

$$K = A\ S^a\ P^b\ e^u \qquad (1)$$

or $\qquad \ln K = \ln A + a \ln S + b \ln P + u \qquad (2)$

where

- $K =$ Net domestic capital formation at 1980-81 prices
- $S =$ Net domestic savings at 1980-81 prices
- $P =$ Population,

and A, a, b are the parameters of the model that are to be estimated, u is the error term and e is the base of the natural logarithm.

Least square regression of net domestic capital formation was run on net domestic savings and population and the exercise yielded the following results

$$\ln (K) = \ln (0.024) + 0.946 \ln (S) + 0.092 \ln (P) \qquad (3)$$
$$(0.114) \qquad (0.330)$$

degrees of freedom = 42

Coefficient of determination = 0.99,

Here the figures in brackets in the second line denote standard error of the coefficients. The fact that the coefficient of determination is very near to unity indicates that equation (3) explains nearly all the variations in the data set. This observation provides the credence to our analysis.

Equation (3) highlights the role of savings in capital formation. Assuming that the rate of growth in population remains unchanged, equation (3) indicates that a unit change in the rate of net domestic savings had resulted, on average, in a change of 0.95 units in the net domestic capital formation. This partial elasticity of net domestic savings to net domestic capital

17

formation has been found to be statistically significant (t= 8.33; d.f.=42; P < .05) implying that capital formation in India has been influenced by the net domestic savings.

By contrast, the rate of net domestic capital formation is nearly inelastic to rate of population increase. The partial elasticity of population has been found to be statistically insignificant (t = 0.28; d.f. = 42; P > .05). This shows that the rate of capital formation in India during 1950-96 has not been influenced by the rate of population increase. Moreover, the elasticity is positive, not negative. This shows that population increase in India, in fact, has contributed towards net domestic capital formation, although in a statistically insignificant manner. This observation is interesting as it has widely been conjectured that rapid population growth has a detrimental effect on capital formation, especially, on the basis of studies carried out during the 1960s. Clearly, the empirical evidence from India for the period1950-96 does not support the view that increase in population size has been detrimental to its economic growth.

Conclusions
Over the years, western economists and development experts have highlighted the negative impact of population growth on economic development through various types of analyses. On the basis of these analyses, they have repeatedly stressed the need to curtail population growth in order to hasten the pace of economic and social development. The present analysis, based on the Indian economic growth data during the period 1950-96, however, indicates that, as far as India is concerned, population and its growth has played only an insignificant role in net domestic capital formation in the country. Even if, this insignificant role is taken to be important then this role has

been towards positive, not negative direction. The very fact that economic growth in India has been largely independent of population related pressure is, itself, a very remarkable feature of the process of economic and social development in India. The Indian experience also indicates that economic growth can remain free from the clutches of population and its pressure through logical economic planning and rational financial management. It also suggests that the addition to the work force as the result of population growth can be utilised in economic development. This implies that a better management of human capital in the form of labour force may also lead to a hastening in the pace of economic development, despite low levels of capital input. In fact, an analysis of the relative contribution of capital, labour and technology on net domestic product has revealed that contribution of both capital and labour in the growth of net domestic product is nearly the same.

The findings of the present analysis have some very important policy implications for economic planning in the developing countries which are facing with the problem of resource crunch. The analysis reveals that it is possible to utilise the available labour force for economic growth through an appropriate mix of human resources development and appropriate production technology which need not to be capital intensive. After all, human force is also a form of the capital. The basic issue is not to reduce this capital for the sake of economic prosperity and development. It may be pointed out here that reduction in birth rate may have some serious implications in terms of availability of labour force in future in the developing countries. In the so called developed countries of the World, today, the greying of population is already posing some serious challenges from social and economic viewpoint as a substantial decline in working age population has been predicted in near future in these countries. The point to be emphasized here is that both capital and labour force are complimentary to each other in the process of economic development and subsequent social transition. In any production process, they cannot replace each other. But the problem with the western economic thought is that it tries to replace labour force by capital inputs, despite the fact that history of economic development in Europe and other developed countries of the World provides ample evidence to confirm that population growth in these countries has been a major contributor to technological advancement which ultimately resulted in high levels of economic growth and advanced levels of social transition. Probably and so obviously, the western economic thought continues to be dominated by the politics of dominance over the developing countries which are poor in technology and capital but rich in labour force.

References

Malthus TR (1798) An *Essay on the Principle of Population as it Affects the Future Improvement of Society*. New York, New Modern Library.

Boserup E (1981) *Population and Technology*. Chicago, Chicago University Press.

Coale AJ and Hoover EM (1958) *Population Growth and Economic Development in Low Income Countries*. Princeton, N.J. Princeton University, Press.

Enke S (1971) Economic consequences of rapid population growth. *Economic Journal*, LXXXI (324): 800-811.

Government ofIndia (1996) *Year Book of Family Welfare Programme in India*. New Delhi, Ministry of Health & Family Welfare.

Government of India (1997) *Economic Survey 1996-97*. New Delhi, Economics Division, Ministry of Finance.

Gopalkrishanan PK (nd) *Notes on our Development Experience since Independence, 1950-85*. Trivandrum, State Planning Board.

Population and Development: The Indian Perspective

Table 1:   Net Domestic Capital Formation, Net
               Domestic Savings and Population Growth in
               India: 1950-96

Year	Net Domestic Capital Formation at current prices (Crore)	Net Domestic Savings at current prices (Crore)	Net Domestic Capital Formation at 1980-81 prices (Crore)	Net Domestic Savings at 1980-81 prices (Crore)	Population (Million)
1950-51	954	975	4501	4600	359
1951-52	1188	1005	5450	4610	365
1952-53	772	806	3704	3867	372
1953-54	909	922	4246	4307	379
1954-55	1070	1054	5587	5503	386
1955-56	1469	1430	7743	7538	393
1956-57	1959	1599	9098	7426	401
1957-58	1843	1370	8253	6135	409
1958-59	1785	1409	7718	6092	418
1959-60	1996	1765	8387	7417	426
1960-61	2544	2063	10468	8489	434
1961-62	2438	2093	9815	8426	444
1962-63	2916	2476	11184	9497	454
1963-64	3266	2826	11487	9939	464
1964-65	3735	3135	12048	10112	474
1965-66	4390	3791	12971	11201	485
1966-67	5437	4514	14250	11831	495
1967-68	5334	4497	12825	10813	506
1968-69	5113	4697	11967	10994	518
1969-70	6285	6044	14274	13727	529
1970-71	7177	6783	16164	15276	541

Capital Formation, Savings and Population Growth

Year	Net Domestic Capital Formation at current prices (Crore)	Net Domestic Savings at current prices (Crore)	Net Domestic Capital Formation at 1980-81 prices (Crore)	Net Domestic Savings at 1980-81 prices (Crore)	Population (Million)
1971-72	7986	7508	17053	16032	554
1972-73	8130	7833	15681	15108	567
1973-74	11824	11432	19422	18778	580
1974-75	13379	12726	19017	18088	593
1975-76	14811	14928	21872	22045	607
1976-77	16721	18030	23150	24962	620
1977-78	18765	20230	24394	26298	634
1978-79	24266	24138	31141	30977	648
1979-80	25278	24698	28184	27537	664
1980-81	30880	28786	30880	28786	679
1981-82	34208	31597	31112	28737	692
1982-83	36340	33774	30661	28496	708
1983-84	41811	39294	32483	30527	723
1984-85	45470	42178	32885	30504	739
1985-86	58167	51933	39230	35026	755
1986-87	61156	54801	38622	34608	771
1987-88	76456	69631	44235	40287	788
1988-89	96972	84668	51968	45374	805
1989-90	114649	102370	56899	50805	822
1990-91	148195	129999	66090	57975	839
1991-92	144113	140736	55946	54635	856
1992-93	169549	155733	60746	55796	872
1993-94	191498	188707	62211	61305	888
1994-95	247804	237840	73285	70339	904
1995-96	300760	281014	83027	77576	920

23

Population and Development: The Indian Perspective

Population Growth and Technology Evolution
An Analysis of Linkages

Introduction

Compared to human history, concern about growth of human population - its determinants and its consequences - may be regarded as a very recent phenomenon. Though, Malthus, two hundred years ago, drew attention of the World towards a possible mismatch between ever growing human population and limitations in increasing the subsistence, yet it was only after 1950, that growth of human population became a common concern in almost all fields of development. Many 'doom's day' scenarios were prescribed and, gradually, a type of consensus emerged which says that human population growth is the root cause of all miseries of the World - a hypothesis which was put forward by Malthus two hundred years ago. One byproduct of this consensus has been increased attention given to the determinants of the population growth. The very first finding that came out at the first stage of analysis was that population growth in the so-called less developed countries of the World was very high. Incidently, many of these countries were and are still extremely poor. As such, without any examination of empirical relationship, there was a general feeling that high rate of population growth and poor social and economic growth go side by side. The Western development experts focussing on this line of thought tried to put forward the argument that the poor social and economic development is a consequence of high population growth. At the same time, there were experts, mainly in the less developed countries who tried to put forward the argument that it is the poor social and economic development which is chiefly responsible for high population growth.

This debate on the linkages between population growth and social and economic development was reflected at its extreme during the World Population Conference at Bucharest in 1974. At the Conference, the whole World was practically divided into two groups - one emphasizing that a reduction in high population growth was an essential precondition for achieving the enhanced levels of social and economic development and the second group focussing on the need for enhancement in the levels of social and economic development and stressing that once enhanced level of social and economic development was achieved it would automatically take care of population growth. There was no consensus at the Conference; nor is there even today. The only change that has taken place today in the debate on population growth and social and economic linkages from the environment in 1974 is that the less developed countries of the World, today, have almost been forced to adopt and implement population control policies by the rich countries of

Europe and North America by attaching conditionalities in the economic aid package which the less developed countries need very urgently for their social and economic development. For example, one essential condition for a country to get assistance from the International Monetary Fund is to initiate population control policies. Such conditionalities have influenced, in a big way, the thinking of the World community about population growth and development linkages.

The social and economic progress of any country, basically, is linked with the development of technology. Here by technology, we mean - in a rather loose sense - the modes of production. As such, the debate on the linkages between population growth and social and economic development may be discussed in the context of population growth and technology development linkages in the World. The key issue, therefore, is whether there is any linkage between technology development and population growth. If yes, then what is the evidence of this linkage, and what is the nature of this linkage. This forms the objective of the present write-up. In order to attempt an answer to this issue, the attention, in this paper, is focussed upon: 1) the evolution of the technology; 2) available theories about population growth and technology development linkages; and 3) the limitations of these linkage. Finally, an attempt has been made to redefine these linkages.

Before proceeding further, an overview of the existing scenario about the linkages between population growth and social and economic development in different countries of the World may be of relevance here. The available evidence suggests that in all those countries - whether less developed or more developed - where an enhanced level of social and economic development has been achieved, the population growth rate has declined substantially. In all the countries of Europe and North America, population growth rates are currently lowest in the World and, in some countries, it is even negative. At the same time, there are some countries and areas in the World which have been able to reduce their population growth rate considerably despite the fat that these countries and areas continue to be poor in the economic sense. Does this mean that a reduction in population growth is not an essential precondition for enhanced social and economic development? In fact, there is considerable difference between what is professed to developing countries in the name of modern development strategy and what is the actual evidence that is available in the World.

Technology Evolution
In recent years, there have been many studies which have tried to explain the evolution of technology in the human history. Archaeological studies have informed us about various stages of human presence on Earth - the stone age, the wood age, the iron age so on. All these ages denote a shift in the main tool of earning subsistence and, therefore, reflect the evolution of technology. The current age - popularly known as the machine age - is of very recent origin. Man did not know the use of machines as a source of power for the production of subsistence before the seventeenth century.

The order of technology evolution since the prehistoric days may be traced from the stone age when the man first learned the use of stones for earning the subsistence by killing animals, digging roots, etc. The stone age was followed by wood age and then iron age. In this process of technology transition, an important feature was development of improved quality of tools for aid to humans. As such, the process of evolution of technology may be said to have been associated with the evolution of man itself on the planet Earth.

Archeologists have different opinions about length of each age. But they are unanimous in stressing that by the period of iron age, the man had developed the ability to produce tools which might help them in securing subsistence under even odd conditions. This means that by the iron age, at least one phase of technology evolution was over. This period was the longest period of human history.

For many years in the human history, nearly all the human efforts have been concentrated simply on increasing the agricultural produce. Attention on non-agricultural produce has been given attention only recently. In order to improve agriculture and to secure enough subsistence for the family and society, man developed many new and improved methods, tools etc. at different points of time. It was in this context that man learned the use of animals in the production process. This use of animal power in the production process was an important milestone in technology evolution as it generated the need for the development of tools and methods which were suitable to animal use. In any case, for the first time, man came to know that he could be replaced in the production process by physically stronger but mentally weaker creatures - animals. It was at this stage, man came to know that he could use his mental power in an even more efficient manner if the physical power part of the production process was assigned to somebody else. It was at this point of time that the man came to know that he could carry out more than one work simultaneously by using his mental prowess. This idea led to the invention of machines and the replacement of animal power in the production process by the machine power.

In the early period of the machine age, man's effort were directed to replace animals in the production process simply because the power available in the animals was also limited. The systems and machines that evolved, therefore, did not replace man but replaced animals. By generating more and more power from the machines, man was able to enhance production considerably. Since, machines required labour for their operation, there was more labour demand, and, therefore, the technologies developed during this period are known as labour intensive technologies. Finally, in the last stage of this evolution process, successful attempts have been made to replace even the labour, at least partially, if not fully, in the production process. Such technologies are termed as labour saving technologies.

But today, the evolution of technology is not related to the quest and efforts related to the survival of the man on the planet Earth. The technology has evolved up to a stage where the man, with a fair degree of surety, can earn his subsistence. The only condition is that the subsistence must be available in the nature. Today, the emphasis in the technology evolution has been more on developing new and more sophisticated modes of consumption of resources that are available on Earth than on securing a minimum that is essential for survival. Unlike the past, today's society is not a subsistence society. Unlike the past, today's economy is not a subsistence economy. Today's society is a society which is oriented towards maximum utilization of the resources. Therefore, the technological development today is more inclined towards creating modes of consumption for utilising the available produce and resources. Since the consumption of primary items like food has a limit, the focus of technology development, today, is on non-agricultural production systems.

Role of Population in Technology Evolution

What has been the role of population - its growth, its size, its distribution - in the process of the evolution of technology? The issue has been a subject of interest to many researches in recent years. However, there is little unanimity among the researches about the linkages of population related factors with technology evolution. There are diverging views.

Boserup says population change has been a major determinant of technological change. She argues that there is a close relationship between population density and food supply system. This close relationship is the result of two long existing processes of adoption. One, population density has adapted to the natural conditions for food production, by migration and by difference in natural rates of population growth. Two, food supply systems have adapted to changes in population density. The essence of her idea is that major determinant of technology evolution is the population density.

Knowell, on the other hand argues that the relatively small size of Britain's population may be regarded as an important factor behind the technology evolution that ultimately led to industrial revolution there. He argues that relatively small size of the country necessitated the development of machines as a substitute for labour to satisfy export market.

But, the population growth did not lead to any technology evolution or industrial revolution in France where the rural population growth rate was very nearly similar to the rural population growth rate in England in the eighteenth century. It is not clear why the factors that led to industrial revolution in England led to mass exodus of labourers from the countryside.

Finally there is the case of less developed countries of the World which are growing at a rapid rate and their population is characterised by all those factors which are conducive to technology evolution according to Boserup's hypothesis. But these countries continue to be technologically very poor. Why, pressure of the population, according to the terminology of Boserup, has failed to generate the process of technology development?

Many explanations have been suggested to explain the above phenomena by extending or by modifying Boserup's ideas. There is no doubt about the fact that man's efforts to secure subsistence for his survival has played a significant role in the evolution of technology throughout the human history. But there is considerable reservation to the hypothesis that man's efforts to secure subsistence or to increase production have led to technology inventions.

I would like to distinguish here between invention and innovation. Invention of a particular concept is the evolving of an idea or thought or fundamental framework which was not known to the World before. Innovation is nothing but application of already known inventions in varied circumstances and situations so as to draw maximum gains from the invention. Invention alone, I would stress, is of very little help to the mankind if it is not applied in an innovative manner to solve prevailing problems and issues.

Thus, it is the combination of invention and innovation that works as a magic in the evolution and popularization of the technology. Invention alone cannot do this magic. What is needed is the innovative application of the invention. This argument can be illustrated with the following example:

The invention of steam as a source of power is attributed to James Watt. But, this invention was of little use to the mankind until George Stevenson applied this power very innovatively in the form of steam engine. Of course, James Watt also tried to develop an engine on the basis of what he invented but his efforts were not innovative enough. The result is that whereas the invention of steam as a power goes to the name of James Watt, the most innovative application of this invention goes to the name of Stevenson.

There is no doubt about the fact that innovations are basically the outcome of human needs, which are best reflected through such variables as population size, population density, population growth rate etc. It is in this context Boserup's hypothesis makes sense. The population pressure has been and continues to be an important factor behind more and more innovative applications of basic or fundamental inventions. But, to say that this population pressure has been the factor behind the invention of a basic or fundamental idea or concept is somewhat far from reality. It is somewhere here that Boserup's hypothesis fails to make sense.

If we look at the circumstances which led to inventions of basic ideas or concepts in the World, we find that majority of these inventions have been spontaneous - by chance. Take the example of steam again. It was by sheer chance that James Watt came to know the hidden power of the steam. The knowledge of the very fact that steam has a driving force did not solve any of the problems of James Watt. But, the knowledge of this very fact that like live creatures in the World, steam also has a driving force opened the avenues for numerous innovative applications of this driving force. These innovative applications of the power of steam, of course, were heavily guided by human demand. There is no doubt about it. What I want to stress upon here is that all the basic inventions in this World have taken place by chance and neither population nor any other factor played any role. This explains why, technological leadership has shifted frequently throughout the human history.

To me, technology evolution at any point of time has at least two components - invention of a basic idea or concept and innovative application of this idea or concept. Population related factors have definitely played a dominating role in the innovative application of the basic or fundamental inventions, at least up to a time in the human history by which international trade had not developed. Once international trade started, it was, and continues to be, the export demand which has been chiefly responsible for the evolution and development of the technology. In the current scenario, it is the international market demand that determines the technology evolution. In fact much of the technology evolution that took place in the form of two industrial revolutions in England can be explained by the simple fact that England, simply by chance came to know the power of the steam which it utilized to meet the demand of the international market. This also explains why technology evolution is not there in the less-developed countries. They do not have an open international market. The only demand which is there is from the domestic sector but the domestic demand is not strong enough for technological innovations and hence for technology evolution.

But as far as the inventions are concerned there is very little evidence to believe that they were the end-results of a long and tedious process of thinking over the problems of mankind in different periods. They may be the outcome of the process of trial and error but in very few cases, these trial and error processes were the outcome of any serious thinking over a particular problem. Rather, many of these process were initiated out of simple curiosity.

To me, therefore, population, its growth and distribution appears to play only a partial role in the evolution and development of the technology and in making the technology more and more efficient and effective by the process of trial and error. Technological inventions, however, seems to be generated only by chance and there was little role of population or any other such factor.

Role of Technology Evolution in Population Growth
Has the evolution of technology and hence better availability of subsistence as the result of the availability of improved technology influenced the growth of population? This question has been addressed in a slightly different form in many studies - in the context of the relationship between population and resources. The classical thinking about this relationship can be

stated in just three words - resources determine population. This means to say that population climbs up to the level permitted by its resource base. Translating the above thinking in the present context, since technology evolution provides better means of production and better availability of subsistence, it can be argued that technology evolution leads to an increase in population.

The above argument holds true, at least in the historical context, up to the period when earning a subsistence to ensure survival was the major challenge to man. In search of better opportunities for earning the subsistence, man, in the prehistoric times, moved from one place to the other and found that there were some places on earth where earning a subsistence was both easier and more secure than other places. This knowledge led to the concentration of population in selected areas. For example, the great Gangatic plains in India has been a very thickly inhabited area since distance past. In fact, all the main civilisation in the past came up in places where earning a subsistence was an easier task. As these highly productive areas attracted more and more people, the population pressure led to innovative application of many inventions that man came to know just by chance. With better use of these inventions, man was able to increase the availability of subsistence thereby attracting people and increasing population further.

Technology evolution led to the increase of population in another way also at least in the pre industrial World. Application of improved technology and increased production demanded more man power. Machines were not there and whatever technology was there it required power for applications. Animals, of course, were there but the need was to control them. This increased demand of manpower resulted in the demand for more children so that more adults were available for work after a certain point of time. Thus, before the appearance of machines on the World map, the technology evolution acted, more or less as an incentive for population growth.

Even during the early phase of industrial revolution, the demand for labour increased considerably since, the technology that was available required enormous man power, as labour input. As a result of increased production, the subsistence, for the first time, was in plenty, much more than the domestic demand and the producers for the first time crossed the domestic market and entered into the international market. But, the demand of the international market was much more than the domestic demand and it was soon found that the existing technology was not efficient enough to cope with this international demand. A major hindrance in meeting the demand was the manpower whose capacity to work was limited. There were innovations to replace man power itself from the production process. These innovations gradually led to labour-saving technology in place of labour intensive technology. This evolution of technology from labour intensive to labour saving phase altered the relationship between technology evolution and population growth. In the pre industrial period, the strength of a nation or a society was judged from its population size or more specifically from the size of its labour force. But after the industrial revolution it was realised that this strength could also be based on the control of machines since machines, by then, had become the main source of production. As a result, capital- machines are nothing but a form of capital - replaced labour in the production process in terms of importance, and there emerged a new paradigm: more capital investment, more production and hence more returns. There was no need of producing more children for labour. Rather, there was a rush for accumulating more and more capital and the technology evolution became independent of population related factors.

We thus found that in the pre industrial World, technology evolution has played a key role in influencing population factors such as its growth, its movement, its distribution etc. But after the innovation of machines, the role of population related factors in technology evolution have diminished considerably. Similarly, in the pre industrial World, population related factors were major influencing factors for technology evolution but new technology evolution is influenced more by capital considerations than by the population related factors. Today, technology evolution is directed to the generation of more and more capital and not for meeting the subsistence needs of the World. The result is that in some parts of the World, there is situation of poverty and hunger and people are living a pitiful life whereas in other parts, huge capital stocks in various forums, have been piled up.

Conditions for Innovation
What are the conditions for technological innovations? Of course, in the pre industrial World, population factors were the most important conditions. But after the industrial revolution, the importance of population related factors in technological innovations has gone down substantially. Today, countries with high population growth and large population have poor technological development while countries with low population

growth have very advanced technological development. As I have mentioned earlier, this change has been due to the increasing importance of capital in the production process. Countries which today have the most advanced technologies, are also the countries which have the largest capital accumulation. They are rich countries of the World. There may be lot of debate on how they became rich by exploiting countries of Africa and Asia during the colonial period but the fact is that they are rich, have large capital accumulation and have utilized this capital for the evolution of technology to an advanced stage. On the other hand the countries with rapidly growing populations are poor in terms of capital and therefore are unable to evolve their technology. They do not have necessary capital required for technology evolution. The conditions for technology innovation have gone a sea change after the industrial revolution. Today, technological change affects population related factors little and is least affected by population related factors. But this was not the situation in the past when the two were very closely linked.

Subsistence vs Market
In the past, at least before the industrial revolution, production was basically oriented towards meeting the domestic demand. Trade usually took place only when there was surplus after meeting the domestic demand and because of the prevailing technological developments, there was little surplus. It got only a secondary importance at that time. Whatever, trade was there, it was usually in the form of exchange not in the form of money or capital. These two factors had promoted the subsistence technology and subsistence economy during those days. In such an economy, almost every family had the knowledge of some type of technological innovation or expertise which the family

members used for earning the subsistence for the family. Market was not a problem because it was not the capital market but exchange market in which one expertise or skill was simply exchangeable to others without any consideration to the relative costs or market value. In such a market, the base of the economy was widely dispersed and every family produced subsistence in one form or the other that was needed by the family. There existed a type of total interdependency among the population groups, one depending on the other for a given commodity while the other depending upon the first for other commodity.

India is perhaps the best example of this economic system of the past. Before the colonial rule, it had a very well diffused knowledge base about various production technologies and it produced wide variety of some very fine goods through the cottage type small industries spread all over the country. Almost every family was producing something which was exchangeable with other commodities in the market. There was practically no role of money or capital in this exchange market. Even, the services were also exchangeable against commodities in this system - a practice which exists even today in many rural areas of the country. In such a system every family contributed to the economy in its own way and, therefore, was self sufficient. Indeed, there was dependancy. But this dependency was a two-way process not the one way process. That was the period when India was known to the World as the Golden Eagle of the East.

But when, the base of the market shifted from exchange to capital or money, the cottage-based technology of India and many other developing countries could not adjust with the situation of the market. Now every commodity had relative capital or money cost which made one commodity cheaper and the other costlier, resulting in favourable or unfavourable terms of trade. More emphasis was given to the production of those commodities which had higher market value than those which had low market value. As a result there was a concentration of capital in few hands or nations who slowly and slowly captured the market. Interdependency was no longer a two-way process. With the over flowing of the market through the machine-made goods, the small enterprises of rural India simply could not compete. Slowly and slowly their goods were pushed out of the market and all the technologies that they knew were simply destroyed.

It is not right to say that this whole process was natural, unbiased. A very significant role in destroying the cottage industry based economic system in India was played by the colonial powers who purposely destroyed the indigenous production system for their own strategic purpose. That is why when Britain prospered in the eighteenth and nineteenth centuries, India - the Golden Eagle of the East was made to starve. It is not known how much of the prosperity of England during the late eighteenth and nineteenth centuries was due to the industrial revolution and how much it was due to the transfer of wealth from India. But, if any such assessment is possible then it will not be surprising to observe that the transfer of wealth from India had played a much dominant role in making England prosperous than the industrial revolution.

Clearly, in modern times, particularly, after the industrial revolution, changes in economic system appear to have played more dominant role than the population pressure in the

41

evolution of technology. This explains why, despite having large population and a heavy population pressure, developing countries of the World today have failed to evolve their own technologies or even to develop further already existing ones.

The Case of Developing Countries

While demographic transition in 18th century England has been tried to be explained in the context of industrial revolution and associated technology evolution, attempts have also been made to explain why technology development has not been able to bring out similar transition in the developing countries of the World. In this section, we focus on the situation in the developing countries.

Most of the population growth that we are witnessing in the developing World today is a recent phenomenon. Two events have been associated with this phenomenon - freedom from colonial powers and eastward sweep of health technology. The process of high population growth can be said to be started with the end of colonial rule. Take the example of India. Till the 1951 census, Indian population never grew more than 1.5 per cent per year. But between 1951 and 1961, the growth of Indian population suddenly and substantially jumped to 1.96 per cent per year. This sudden jump in the population growth rate has been attributed to the implementation of large scale health programmes equipped with latest health technology which brought down the death rates substantially while there was practically no change in the birth rate. Interestingly, and quite conspicuously, the British during their rule in India, attempted least to improve the living conditions in the country. They never tried to put into practice the health technology that was developed by them. It was only after the Independence that the health technology showed its effect.

It is important to note here that this health technology which resulted in a sharp decline in death rate and hence in a sharp rise in population size was not developed in India. It was imported one. As a result it had only a limited impact. It definitely reduced the death rate but did not improve the living conditions. Here, it may be pointed out that in the developed countries, reduction of death rates was not due to the application of health technology but due to proper housing etc. For example, by the time measles was eradicated in England, no measles vaccine was developed.

It is clear that the demographic transition achieved in the western countries has been associated with an overall improvement in living conditions. In the developing countries, while the effect of health technology in bringing down death rates was substantial there was no associated improvement in living conditions. The birth rate, the morbidity rate, etc. remain high simply because improvements in living conditions require heavy social investment which is not there because of the inappropriate functioning of the economy. Now the effect of health technology on population growth appears to have diminished as may be seen from stagnation in death rates in may countries simply because, to be effective, the health technology itself requires parallel development in social and economic context. The same is true for fertility control technology that was heralded in the developing countries around 1965. Again, it would be worthwhile to mention that, the birth rate in Europe and England declined well before the evolution of modern contraceptive technology.

Conclusions

There is no doubt that, in the past, population pressure and population growth might have played a very important role in the evolution and development of the technology. At least up to the eighteenth century, the relationship between population growth and technology evolution appears to be very strong and unambiguous. That was the period when the evolution of the technology was very linked to the survival of the man, at least in Europe, where conditions for survival were extremely poor at that time. Unfortunately, very little is known for other areas of the World about such relationships as most of the studies on population and technology linkage are based upon European experience. For example, when Europe was struggling for survival, India was passing through its golden phase of economic and social prosperity. It is not known whether the prosperity of India during that period was due to population pressure or due to other social and economic structures.

In any case, the relationship between population growth and pressure and technology evolution which was so unambiguous in Europe in the past, especially, at the time of the industrial revolution is no longer clear today, especially in the developing countries of the World. The reason is that, in recent years, development and evolution of the technology do not appear to be guided at all by population related issues. Rather, capital gains appear to be playing a much more dominant role in influencing the development and evolution of the technology. In other words, the human welfare orientation of technology evolution and development of the past has now been replaced by the orientation towards capital formation and capital gains. This shift in the basic orientation has also resulted in more attention towards the development of capital intensive rather than labour intensive technology and in making the whole process of technology development and technology evolution a very highly capital intensive process - beyond the reach of the poor. Population pressure, virtually, has no influence in such a situation.

In the past, large populations were symbols of power and strength. Today, it is the capital which has become the symbol of strength and might. Perhaps the most critical issue with the evolution and development of technology is that it has always been associated with the desire to rule the World.

Population and Development: The Indian Perspective

Demand And Supply of Food in India: 1950-2000

Introduction

Concern about feeding the growing human population may be regarded as old as the presence of man on Earth. The reason is simple - food is essential for the survival of man. Ensuring food to population has been seen as the prime reason behind the changes in behavioural and settlement patterns in the World. Boserup has discussed, in detail, these patterns and linked these changes with the growth of human population (Boserup, 1981). The earlier thinking on the relationship between population and food was that population climbed up to the level permitted by its food base. Reflections of this view may be seen in Botero's statement that human population did not grow because environmental resources were insufficient to support a larger population (Botero, 1588). Sir Walter Raleigh in 1650 also noted that although Spain sent large number of people to war,

47

the size of the country's population remained stationary. This, he attributed to the fact that Spain's population was adjusted to what the country could nourish (Raleigh, 1650). Some of the early writings of Malthus, especially his first essay, also expresses this view.

The classical thinking that resources determine population has support in the patterns of population growth in Europe during the Eighteenth century. It has been argued that the increase in food supply as the result of industrial revolution allowed rapid population growth. Introduction of mechanisation to cultivation and harvesting, together with the widespread use of chemical fertilisers had enabled man to increase food production substantially and to provide for considerably larger population that was heretofore possible (Lio, et. al 1979).

The basic issue, today, is related with the man's potential to increase food production to meet the needs of continuously growing population. There are both pessimistic as well as optimistic views. According to optimists, the classical thinking about population and food has a basic flaw. It conceives man as essentially an inert creature - responding to changes in resources but initiating nothing (Keyfitz, 1984). In fact, the man is the wisest creature on the planet Earth and it is simply naive to presume that man initiates nothing.

The pessimists, on the other hand, raise serious doubts about man's ability to produce more food in future mainly because of two counts. First they argue that almost all the cultivable land on Earth has been utilised and there is little scope for increasing the cultivated area any further. Second increased food production from the currently developed arable lands has its limits in the long run. It is therefore feared that limitations to the increase in food production may bring in a gap between the demand and supply of food in the World.

The current patterns of growth in population and increase in food supply for the World provides an evidence which does not support the pessimists fear of worldwide food shortages. Studies carried out by United Nations Food and Agricultural Organisation show that for the World as a whole, the total food production is sufficient, even at the low technological input levels, to provide an adequate nutritious diet to the present World population and that growth in World food production can remain abreast of projected World population growth (FAO, 1984). But the scenario changes drastically when we look into the issue in regional or in country context. Problems vary widely. Africa, for example, has the land but its population is growing at such a fast rate that it is not possible to meet the food needs of the population that is added every year from the current levels of production. Even more alarmingly, in a number of African countries in which population growth is steadily increasing over the past two decades, food consumption per person has fallen below minimum nutritional requirements (Economic Commission for Africa, 1984).

In South Asia, the issues involved are different. In this region, nearly all the arable land has been utilised for agriculture (Revelle, 1984). Future increases in food production in this part of World will depend crucially on the productivity of land. Thus, while in Africa, the major issue is how to feed the existing rapidly growing population; in South Asia, the issue that is of prime concern is how to maintain, if not to increase, the rate of growth of food production so as to meet out the food demand.

It is in the foregoing background, we analyse and discuss population and food related issues in India - the second most populous country of the World. The Indian record of meeting food needs of its population is a mix of ups and downs. In the early days of Independence, food production in the country was more than enough to meet the food needs of its population. In late sixties and early seventies, however, the domestic food production slumped drastically because of a number of exogenous as well as endogenous factors. This slump in the food production resulted in heavy food imports at a considerable national cost - in terms of both money and prestige. Today, the country is a food surplus country. This, however, does not mean that food problems of the country are over. The food balance in the country continues to be a delicate one and future trends in meeting the food demand will depend largely upon what action is taken now.

Demand For Food in India: 1950-90
Estimation of the demand for food in a country like India is very tricky. India is a vast country with extreme diversities. It is not surprising that the dietary patterns in the country very widely between different geopolitical regions and socio-cultural groups. These dietary patterns suggest that the country can be divided into at least three zones as far as the broad pattern of the composition of diet is concerned - the north and north western part where diet is wheat based, the eastern part where the diet is rice based and the western part where the diet is wheat and millet based. However, one common feature of dietary patterns in India is that they are primarily of legume

culture and so the major proportion of the diet is constituted by cereals throughout the country.

Because of the above pattern of diet composition in almost all parts of the country, we have confined ourselves to the estimation of total food grains demand only. Focus on the demand for food grains is justified from the nutrition viewpoint also. In India, nearly all the malnutrition that prevails in the country is the protein calorie malnutrition. Since food grains provide the bulk of the calorie contents of the diet, it is logical to explore the demand in terms of food grains only. Mitra (1982) has suggested that if the food grains needs of the population are met then it will go a long way in meeting other nutritional needs of the population.

Two approaches are generally used for estimating demand for food. The first approach is the normative approach. In this approach, the minimum food needs of a reference person are estimated through standard procedures and, on the basis of this norm, the food demand for the whole population is calculated. The norms to be used for the estimation of the food demand may be derived in two forms. In the first form, the norm is expressed in terms of minimum calorie needs for different population groups. Such norms have been extensively used by the United Nations Food and Agricultural Organisation for estimating the food demand in different countries of the World. According to this organisation, the minimum calorie needs of an Indian reference person is estimated to be 2210 Kcal per day (FAO, 1984).

In the second form of the normative approach of estimating food demand, minimum needs of a reference person in terms of calories, vitamins, etc. are taken into consideration. This approach is commonly used in the Indian planning process. The estimation of food demand by the Planning Commission of India is based on this approach.

The demand for food, however, is not the same in all the age groups as well as for males and females. On the other hand, among females, pregnant women and lactating mothers have higher and specific food demand than other women. Recognising this fact, Gopalan and others have estimated average food requirements for different age groups of the population and separately for males and females (Gopalan, et. al 1971). The minimum daily food grains requirement for persons of different age groups as obtained by Gopalan and others are compiled in table 1. From this table the average per capita food demand can be calculated once the age and sex structure of the population is known. For India, the information on age and sex structure of the population is available through different population censuses.

The normative approach suggested by Gopalan and others has been used in this paper to estimate the demand for food grains in the country since 1950. According to the estimates prepared by Gopalan, total demand for food grains in the country during 1950 was about 56.12 million tonnes - 49.46 million tonnes cereals and 6.66 million tonnes pulses. By 1990, this demand increased to approximately 133.34 million tonnes - 115.07 tonnes of cereals and 18.27 million tonnes of pulses. In other words, over a duration of 40 years, the demand for food grains in the country increased by more than 77 million tonnes. During the decade 1950-60, the food grains demand in the country increased by 11.69 million tonnes. This figure, during

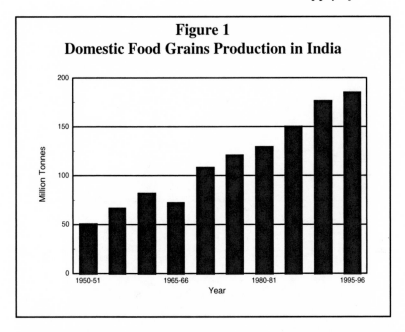

Figure 1
Domestic Food Grains Production in India

1960-70, was 20.28 million tonnes and 26.05 million tonnes during 1970-80. During the decade 1980-90, the increase in food grains demand decreased because of a slow down in the growth of population. Compared to 1970-80, the increase in food grains demand during eighties was about 20.20 million tonnes.

Food Supply in India

There are two determinants of food supply - domestic food production and food import. It is in the context of food supply that self-sufficiency in domestic production has been and continues to be a long cherished dream of many countries including India. The reason is simple. Over the years, food imports throughout the World have been associated with increasing political pressures and even assaults. Food surplus

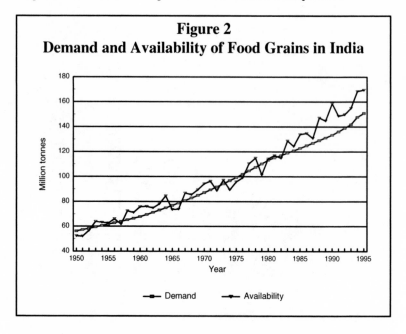

Figure 2
Demand and Availability of Food Grains in India

nations have shown a tendency of using the surplus food they have as a political arsenal in meeting their own interests. Further, because of the fact that most of the food production in the World is confined to a few nations, the prices in the World food grains market have increased making for the already extremely poor countries of the World almost impossible to purchase the food grains at prevailing market prices. India also had the experience of the indignity caused by food import when it signed an agreement for food imports at reduced prices with the United States of America.

Not all the food that is produced in the farm is available for human consumption. A part of it is consumed through the nonhuman use or is wasted. Moreover, a proportion of the domestic production is retained by the government to maintain a buffer stock in order to meet the exigencies. The net food grains available for consumption, therefore, is less than the total food produced. On the other hand, government imports food to meet the demand for food in the country. Total food available, thus, may be obtained by adjusting the production for wastage, animal feed etc. as well as for the imports, if any. As such, the discussion on trends in the availability of food grains in the country is preceded by a discussion on the trends in domestic food production and food import.

a. Food Production in India: 1950 to 1990

The Indian record of domestic food production is a mixed success story. Today, India has a huge buffer stock of food grains. Looking into the enormous size of the country and the diversities which are associated with such a big population, this near self-sufficiency in food production in India may be regarded as an achievement of supreme order. The value of this achievement increases all the more because of the fact that in a number of developing countries of the World, the problems related to the feeding of their populations has increased over time.

During the past 40 years, food grains production in India has recorded an almost three-time increase - from about 50.89 million tones to more than 176 million tones. In between 1950 and 1960, the food production in India increased by about 31 million tonnes. In the decade 1960-70, this increase was about 26.4 million tonnes which decreased further to 21.1 million tonnes during the decade 1970-80. But during the decade 1980-90, food production in the country increased by 46.8 million tonnes.

Most of the increase in food grains production has, however, been confined to cereals, and that too, to wheat and rice. Increase in the production of pulses, the main supplier of protein in the Indian diet, has contributed to even less than 4 per cent of the total increase in food grains production in the country. In the 40 years between 1950 and 1990, production of pulses in the country increased from 8 million tonnes to 12.5 million tones - an increase of only 4.5 million tonnes. Production of pulses in the country, however, was lowest in the year 1980 when only 7.6 million tonnes of pulses could be produced.

Among cereals, highest average annual growth rate has been recorded in wheat while the growth rate in coarse grains has been quite low and even negative in some cases. At the aggregate level, increase in coarse grains was only about 11 per cent of the total increase in the food grains production. The rest of the increase was almost equally divided between wheat and rice.

b. Food Imports: 1950 to 1990
During the early days of Independence, India was a regular importer of food grains despite the fact that food supply from domestic production was sufficient to meet the domestic food grains demand. However, the quantity of the import was almost insignificant to the quantity of total domestic production. During the period 1950 to 1955, total food grains import in India was only 13.4 million tonnes while the domestic food grains production during the same period was almost 367 million tonnes. In 1956, Government of India made an agreement with the United States of America which is popularly known as PL-480. Under this agreement, India

imported food grains and other agricultural produce at a confessional rate with an intention of building a buffer stock for security against exogenous risks.

But this availability of imported food grains was followed by a series of bad crop years. The domestic food production fell dramatically and the imported food grains became the mainstay of the public distribution system. The dependency on imported food grains to meet the food grains demand increased considerably and the country had to import more than 10 million tonnes of food grains in 1966 alone. During the period 1966 to 1970, the country imported more than 32 million tonnes of food grains to meet the food demand of the country.

In any case, food grains import has never been a major contributor to meeting the food grains demand in the country. At its peak, total food grains import was even less than 10 per cent of the total domestic production. During the period 1971-1975, total food grains import decreased to 18.3 million tonnes and, after 1976, food grains import became negligible to total domestic food grains production largely because of significant increase in the domestic food grains production.

c. Food Balance: 1950 to 1990
It is now possible to discuss the food balance in the country during the past 40 years. The food balance may be defined as the difference between the net availability of food grains minus the food grains demand.

During the early years of Independence, up to 1958, the food balance in the country was negative implying that the demand for food was more than the availability of food either through domestic production or through food imports. In the year 1950, for example, the demand for food was 56.12 million tonnes while the availability of food was only 52.3 million tonnes. From 1959 onwards, the food balance in the country turned positive but because of severe drought conditions during 1966 and 1967, the domestic food production fell considerably and food balance turned negative again. A similar situation existed during the period 1973-77 also when, because of the erratic monsoon, the domestic production of food grains again fell considerably. However, since 1980, there has been a considerable increase in the domestic food grains production in the country with the result that the country has now turned a food surplus country instead of a food deficit country as was the case in the past. By 1990, net food availability in the country was 144.8 million tonnes against the estimated food demand of 133.34 million tonnes - a surplus of 11.46 million tonnes.

The balance in terms of cereals and in terms of pulses, is however different. In the early years of Independence, the balance in terms of cereals was negative while that of the pulses was positive. In recent years, the pattern has reversed - the balance in terms of cereals is now positive implying that the country is producing more than the demand but the food balance in terms of pulses has turned negative. In 1990, the demand for cereals in the country was estimated to be approximately 115 million tonnes, against which the total cereals availability was 132.3 million tonnes. On the other hand, the demand for pulses, in 1990, was approximately 18.27 million tonnes against which the availability was only 12.5 million tonnes - a deficit of almost six million tonnes. Interestingly, the gap between the demand and availability of pulses in the country has increased over time. Clearly, the food supply in the country is imbalanced. This imbalance is the result of over emphasis on cereals and neglect of pulses in domestic food grains production.

Projections of Food Grains Demand
The task of projecting the food grains demand for future is even more arduous than analysing the past trends. It is very likely that the conclusions arrived at the end may be having a substantially high probability of being not realised at all. The reason is simple. An estimation of future demand depends not only on the current state of affairs but also on the future shape of things to come. As such, projection is basically a guided outcome of the assumption that are assumed before hand and therefore its relevancy should be evaluated only in the context of these assumptions.

Any projection of food demand requires, as a precondition, a projection of the population.

a. Future Growth of Indian Population
At the time of 1991 population census, the population of the country was enumerated to be 846.3 million. This count is presumed to be associated with an error of undercount, which normally is small. Taking into consideration this error due to undercount, United Nations has estimated that, in 1990, the population of the country was 850.6 million. Using this estimate of population of the country, United Nations has made three projections for the future population growth of the country - the high, medium and low variants. According to the medium variant population projections prepared by the United Nations, the population of the country is expected to increase

to 935.7 million by 1995 and to 1022 million by the turn of the century (United Nations, 1996). The Planning Commission, on the other hand, has projected a population of about 1003 million by the turn of the century (Government of India, 1996).

Projection of the population of the country has also been worked out by the author. It has been assumed in the projection exercise that the replacement level fertility will be achieved in the country by the year 2010. Three variations in fertility decline have been used - 1) a slow initial decrease in the total fertility rate; 2) a linear decrease in the total fertility rate; and 3) an exponential decrease in the total fertility rate. Under the first assumption of future fertility decline, the population of the country is expected to reach 1034 million by the turn of the century, a figure very close to the high variant projection of United Nations. On the other hand, if it is assumed that the fertility will follow the past linear declining trend in future also, then the population of the country has been projected to reach 1014 million by the turn of the century. Finally, if it is assumed that the total fertility rate decline in future will follow an exponential trend, then the population of the country is projected to increase to 1008 million by the turn of the century.

An analysis of the trend in the total fertility rate during the period 1980 through 1990 has revealed that total fertility rate in the country had decreased almost linearly during the decade. If it is assumed that this trend will continue in future - at least in the near future - also, then it can be assumed that the population of the country is expected to reach around 1014 million by the turn of the current century. However, if it is assumed that the fertility decline will gain momentum in the years to come as the result of official efforts, then, one may expect a relatively slower growth in the population of the country. In this alternatively scenario, the population of the country is expected to reach 1008 million by the turn of the century.

An analysis of the trend in the total fertility rate during the period 1980 through 1990 reveals that the total fertility rate in the country has declined almost linearly. If it is assumed that this trend will continue in future also then it is estimated that the population of the country will be around 1014 million by the turn of the Century.

B. Future demand for food

Once the estimated size of the population of the country by the year 2000 is known, it is possible to estimate the demand for food by applying the norms suggested by Gopalan and others. These estimates are given in table 4. They suggest that the net food grains requirement for the human population of the country, at the turn of the century, will be in between 161.82 and 162.38 million tonnes depending upon whether population of the country reaches 1008 million or 1014 million. If a wastage factor of ten per cent is also taken into consideration, then gross food grains requirement for the country is expected to be around 180 million tonnes by the turn of the century. This food grains demand is for human consumption only. It does not taken into consideration the food grains demand for animal consumption.

It may, however, be pointed out that the above food demand has been estimated on the basis of minimum food grains required to meet the minimum calorie requirements of an average individual. It does not take into consideration the income elasticity of food grains demand. It is well known that the food grains demand increases with the increase in per capita income. This increase is rapid at low and middle income levels but slows down rapidly as the per capita income increases. At very high levels of the per capita income, it has been observed that the demand for food grains is virtually inelastic to the level of per capita income. However, the demand of food grains required for ensuring that the minimum calorie requirements of an average individual are met remains unchanged as this demand is independent of the level of per capita income.

Prospects for Food Grains Supply
An assessment of the future food grains supply prospects is even more formidable than projecting the food grains demand. The reason is that food grains supply is more sensitive to exogenous factors than the food grains demand. Moreover, both population and economic growth have a certain inherent continuity which makes it possible to project them with some degree of certainty, at least for the near future. But the yield of agriculture produce which is one of the proximate determinants of food grains production does not have this inherent continuity. It may go up and down because of the climatic variations which is usually the case. Perhaps the most crucial role is played by the technological advancement but putting technological advancement in the quantitative terms is the most difficult task.

Area under cultivation and yield may be regarded as the only proximate determinants of food grains production. An analysis of the pattern of change in these determinants that has been experienced in the past, therefore, may be helpful in formulating possible trends in future which may be of some aid in assessing future food grains supply. In fact, in all eventuality, it is the past experience which guides us to peep into the future.

During the 45 years between 1950 and 1995, area under food grains in the country increased from 97.321 million hectares in 1950 to 123.5 million hectares in 1995. This amounts to an increase of about 26.18 million hectares or an increase of almost 27 per cent from the area under cultivation in 1950. This means that on average, area under food grains in the country recorded a growth rate of 0.6 per cent per year. This increase, however, was not uniform throughout the period. Increase in the area was highest during the decade 1950-60 when the area under food grains cultivation recorded an increase of more than 18 million hectares. During the decade 1960-70, this increase reduced to 8.70 million hectares and to only 2.40 million hectares during 1970-80. In between 1980 and 1990, area under food grains cultivation increased by only 1.1 million hectares but in between 1990 and 1995, this area, instead of increasing, decreased by about 4.3 million hectares. This implies that the area under food grains cultivation in the country has reached its limit and there is very little scope of increasing the area any further. In other words, any further increase in the food grains production in the country cannot be ensured through the increase in the area under food grains cultivation. Clearly, any future increase in the food grains production in the country will crucially depend upon the increase in the yield of different food grains. It can, therefore, be assumed that area under food grains will play only an insignificant role in projecting food grains supply in future.

By contrast, productivity of the land increased substantially in the past 45 years - from 522 kg/hectare in 1950 to 1548 kg/hectare in 1994. In 1995, the yield decreased slightly to 1499 kg/hectare. In other words, food grains yield, on average, recorded a growth of 4.37 per cent per year during the last 45 years. Once again, and expectedly, the increase in the food grains yield was not uniform. In between 1950 and 1960, the food grains yield increased by 188 kg per hectare; during 1960 and 1970, it increased by 162 kg per hectare and in between 1970 and 1980, the increase was of the order of 151 kg per hectare. However, during the decade 1980 through 1990, the increase in food grains yield was very rapid - 357 kg per hectare. In between 1990 and 1994 also, the food grains yield in the country increased very rapidly.

It would be of interest to analyse here, how much of the increase in the food grains production in the country during the last 45 years has been due to the increase in area under food grains cultivation and how much of the increase has been due to the increase in the yield of food grains. For this purpose, we have applied the decomposition methodology. The analysis suggests that the increase in the area under cultivation in the country during the past 45 years has accounted for only about 20 per cent of the total increase in food grains production while more than four fifth of the total increase in food grains production has been accounted by the increase in the productivity of the land or the yield of the produce. It has also been observed that the contribution of the increase in area in increasing the food grains production has decreased over time and has even turned negative in recent years. Increase in area under food grains accounted for almost 36 per cent of the total increase in food grins production between 1950 and 1960. This proportion reduced to 26 per cent between 1960 and 1970; to almost 11 per cent between 1970 and 1980; and to just 2.83 per cent between 1980 and 1990. Between 1990 and 1995, the contribution of increase in area to the increase in food grains production turned negative because of a decrease in the area. In between 1990 and 1995, the food grains production in the country increased by about 8.8 million tonnes. Had there been no decrease in the area, the increase in the production of food grains would have been of the order of almost 15 million tonnes. This shows that, in recent years, all the increase in the production of food grains in the country may be attributed to the increase in the yield of different foods grains and not to the increase in the area under cultivation. In fact, there is little scope of any further increase in the area under food grain cultivation in the country and any future increase in the food grains production will depend upon the food grains yield.

Given the above situation, three scenarios can be projected for the yield of food grains for the year 2000 AD. In the first scenario, average yield of food grains is expected to increase by 50 kg per hectare per year so as to reach the 1800 kg per hectare by the turn of the century. On the other hand, if a rapid increase in the yield is assumed than the average yield of food grains is expected to reach 1900 kg per hectare by the turn of the century. But if it is assumed that the increase in the yield will be slow, then it can be assumed that average yield of food grains will be about 1700 kg per hectare by the turn of the century.

As far as the area under food grains production is concerned, at least two scenarios can be projected. In the first scenario, the area under food grains is expected to remain about 124 million hectares; in the second scenario, it is assumed that the current preference for cash crops is expected to result in a decrease in the area under food grains by about 4 million hectares by the turn of the century.

On the basis of the above assumptions, total production of food grains in the country, at the turn of the century, is expected to be between 204 million tonnes and 235.6 million tonnes depending upon the area under food grains cultivation and levels of the yield of food grains. Under the most likely situation of a decrease of about 4 million hectares in the area under food grains cultivation and an average food grains yield of 1800 kg per hectare, total food grains production in the country in expected reach 216 million tonnes by the turn of the century. If it is assumed that of the total food grains produced, about 10 per cent will be wasted in transportation and storage and for animal consumption, the total availability of food grains in the country by the turn of the century is expected to be 194.40 million tonnes. Given the estimated gross food demand of approximately 180 million tonnes, this implies that, under the normal conditions, the food balance in the country is expected to remain positive up to the turn of the century with a buffer stock of approximately 14 million tonnes. This means that under the most likely scenario of a medium variant projection of population and a normal pattern and trend of food grains production, the country is expected to remain a food surplus country in the next century.

Conclusions
The foregoing analysis provides ample evidence to suggest that through persistent efforts and technological innovations, India has been able to avoid the Malthusian trap and has turned from a food deficit country to a food surplus country. Moreover, there is ample evidence to suggest that in future also, the

country will be able to feed its increasing population at its own, without any food imports. Obviously, the pressure of an increasing population has been one of the guiding factors behind sustained efforts for increasing food grains production in the country.

The realisation of the food balance projected in this analysis, however depends crucially upon the extent up to which it is possible to provide inputs into the agriculture sector. In this context, it may be pointed out that in the early days of Independence, India opted for a development strategy and a development planning process based on the concept of promotion of industrialisation. It was thought at that time that the benefits of industrialisation will ultimately result in the modernisation of and increased inputs into the agriculture sector. But this trickle down phenomenon did not take place and when food import at the concessional rates was not possible there were wide-ranging problems. This experience led the government to change its policy towards agriculture and increasing agricultural production became a priority issue in development planning.

But even the first phase of the so-called green revolution was not very much successful in solving the food related problems. By 1976-77, there were unmistakable sings that the green revolution did not benefit the small and marginal farmers at all. Their production remained stagnant at low levels depending upon the uncertainties of nature. It was also clear by that time that the deteriorating effect of mass poverty was a major obstacle in enhancing agricultural production as small and marginal farmers were not having necessary resources that might be put into agriculture to boost production. There was then considerable wisdom about how to support these small and marginal farmers so that they may increase their income mainly through increase in agricultural production. This wisdom resulted in the form of what are now known as beneficiaries oriented development programmes. These programmes focus on helping the poor in the form of both technical as well as monetary inputs so that they can raise the productivity of their assets. Since land is the main asset of majority of the population in the country, a major implication of these efforts have been a boost in the agricultural production which is visible in the trend in food grains production after 1980.

Major improvement in food grains production in India, therefore, may be seen in the efforts to reach the poor - the small and marginal farmers who constitute the bulk of the productive force. Providing them with the latest knowledge and enhancing their resources through both skill development and capital assistance have been the key to increase agricultural productivity in India. These efforts at the beneficiaries level have been ably supported through prices support system, well-developed procurement network and a very advanced research and development organisation. All these efforts have transformed a food deficit country of early sixties and late seventies into a food surplus country in the eighties. Today the strength of the agriculture sector in India is such that the country has been able to withhold the effects of severe drought that plagued most parts of the country around 1987-88.

The foregoing projection exercise does not take into consideration the income elasticity of food grains demand. It may be expected that increase in the per capita income may lead to an increase in per capita demand for food grains but there is a possibility that increase in per capita income will also result in agricultural productivity through increased investments in agriculture.

References

Botero G 1589 (1956) *The Reason of State*. Translated and edited by PJ Waley and DP Waley. New Heaven, Yale University Press.

Economic Commission for Africa (1984) Food production and population growth in Africa. In United Nations *Population. Resources, Environment and Development*. New York, United Nations.

Food and Agricultural Organisation (1984) Population, resources and development. In United Nations, opp. cit.

Food and Agricultural Organisation (1984) *The State of Food and Agriculture*. Rome, FAO.

Gopalakrishnan PK (1986) *Notes on Our Development Experience Since Independence*. 1950-85. Trivandrum, State Planning Board.

Gopalan, C. and others (1971) *Diet Atlas of India*. Hyderabad, National Institute of Nutrition.

Government of India (1996) *Yearbook of National Family Welfare Programme*. New Delhi, Ministry of Health and Family Welfare.

Population and Development: The Indian Perspective

Keyfitz N (1984) Impact of trends in resources, environment and development on demographic process. In United Nations (1984) opp. cit.

Lio K, Hirooka T, Kato S (1979) *Population Growth and Food Problems in Selected Asian Countries.* New York, United Nations Fund for Population Activities.

Mitra A (1982) Population growth and food supply. In United Nations: *Population of India.* Bangkok, Commission for Asia and Pacific.

Raleigh Sir W (1650) Cited in RL Smith (1966) *Ecology and Field Biology.* New York, Harper and Row.

Revelle R (1984) The effect of population growth on renewable resources. In United Nations (1984) *Population. Resources, Environment and Development.* New York, United Nations.

United Nations (1994) *World Population Prospects.* New York, United Nations.

Table 1:   Daily food grains requirements for different age groups in India.

Age	Average food grains required per day (gm)		
	Cereals	Pulses	Total
1-3 years	150	46	196
4-6 years	200	53	253
7-9 years	250	63	313
10-12 years	320	63	383
13-14 years	395	56	451
15-18 years	395	56	451
Non-pregnant and non-lactating females	375	56	431
Pregnant females	425	56	481
Lactating females	475	66	541
Adult males	508	66	574

Source: Gopalan et. al (1971)

Population and Development: The Indian Perspective

Table 2: The food grains balance in India: 1950-90. (Million tonnes)

Year	Commodity	Demand	Availability	Balance
1950	Food grains	56.12	52.30	-3.82
	Cereals	49.46	44.30	-5.16
	Pulses	6.66	8.00	1.34
1960	Food grains	67.81	71.20	3.39
	Cereals	58.12	60.80	2.68
	Pulses	9.69	10.40	0.71
1970	Food grains	87.09	89.50	2.41
	Cereals	74.94	79.30	4.36
	Pulses	12.15	10.20	-1.95
1980	Food grains	113.14	101.40	-11.74
	Cereals	98.06	93.80	-4.26
	Pulses	15.09	7.60	-7.49
1990	Food grains	133.34	144.80	11.46
	Cereals	115.07	132.30	17.23
	Pulses	18.27	12.50	-5.77

Table 3:   Project population growth in India.
                (Million)

Year	Source	High	Medium	Low
1995	UN	938.422	935.744	933.037
	GOI		924.000	
	Author	938.888	933.063	931.215
2000	UN	1030.545	1022.021	1013.445
	GOI		1003.000	
	Author	1033.747	1014.050	1008.018

Table 4:   Projected food grains demand in India.
                 (Million tonnes)

Year		Cereals	Pulses	Total
1995	High	128.07	20.21	148.29
	Medium	127.66	20.11	147.77
	Low	127.53	20.08	147.61
2000	High	141.94	22.27	164.22
	Medium	140.48	21.90	162.38
	Low	140.03	21.78	161.82

Table 5:   Projected domestic food grains production in
                 India by the year 2000 AD.
                 (Million tonnes)

Project yield (Kg/hectare)	Project area (Million hectares)	
	124.00	120.00
1700	210.80	204.00
1800	223.20	216.00
1900	235.60	228.00

World Commercial Energy Use Patterns: 1980-94

Introduction

In recent years, there has been a nearly universal acceptance of the view that various links exist between population, environment and economic phenomena. However, the nature and strength of the relationship among the three continue to be the subject of heated debate. While some studies have asserted that population growth is not an obstacle to economic growth, others support the conclusion that population growth has strong negative impact on the environment. It is argued that as population growth adds to consumers who put additional claims to natural resources, and produced pollution, it damaged environment. Conversely, deterioration of the environment damaged the economy (United Nations, 1993). In the literature concerning population, economy and environment, the interaction between the population, consumption (or production) patterns and technology, as they affect environment is often encapsulated by the simple equation

$$I = PAT$$

where I is the environmental impact, P is the population, A is per capita consumption and T is a measure of environmental damage done by the available technology in supplying each unit of consumption. At its face value, this equation implies that consumption or production patterns are proximate determinants of changes in the environment, channelling the underlying impacts of ultimate causes, which are the number of consumers and their effective demands and services.

Although, the above simple relationship between population, economy and environment has been questioned primarily because of its simplicity, yet this relationship does provide a simple framework for an empirical analysis of the interaction between population and consumption patterns at a given level of technology as they affect environment. It may be seen from the above equation that the product P.A is the total consumption (or production) at a given level of technology. In other words, at a given level of technology, the environmental impact is directly proportional to total consumption. An analysis of the trends and patterns in consumption, therefore, provides an interesting opportunity to explore the environmental dimensions of population and development.

Sources of data
In this paper, information on commercial energy use for two time periods spaced 15 years apart - 1980 and 1994 - for 118 countries of the World both developing and developed has been

utilized to analyse trends and patterns in consumption between 1980 and 1994. This information is available from the World Bank data bank on key development indicators of member countries (World Bank, 1997). The information on total commercial energy use available from the World Bank refers to domestic primary energy use before transformation to other end-use fuels (such as electricity and refined petroleum products). It also includes products for non-energy uses, mainly derived from petroleum. These estimates, however, do not include energy estimates of use of firewood, dried animal excrement and other traditional fuels despite the fact that these traditional sources of energy are quite substantial in some developing countries (World Bank, 1997).

The World Bank groups its member countries into four categories on the basis of the gross national product per capita - low income economies (LIE), lower middle income economies (LMIE), upper middle income economies (UMIE) and high income economies (HIE). Out of the 118 countries included in this analysis, 47 are low income economies; 30 are lower middle income economies; 15 are upper middle income economies and 26 are high income economies. Although, the two most populous countries of the World, China and India, are included in the LIE category, World Bank prefers to present the data for these two countries separately from the rest of low income economies of the World.

Following the classification adopted by the World Bank, the analysis here has been carried out separately for low income economies, India, China, lower middle income economies, upper middle income economies and high income economies. The reason for carrying out analysis separately for each group is simple; the economies differ widely in terms of population growth as well as in terms of per capita consumption.

Trends and Patterns in Commercial Energy Use

In the year 1980, according to the World Bank estimates, total commercial energy use in the 118 countries included in this analysis was of the order to 5.212 billion metric tones of oil equivalent which increased to 6.892 billion metric tones of oil equivalent in the year 1994. This means that during the 15 years period between 1980 and 1994, total commercial energy use in the 118 countries increased by an absolute amount of 1.681 billion metric tones of oil equivalent. In relative terms, this implies an increase of 32.24 per cent from the level of 1980. In other words, the total commercial energy use in the 118 countries of the World increased at an average annual geometric rate of increase of 1.88 per cent per year.

Rate of increase in the commercial energy use has, however, been not uniform in all countries. In the high income economies, increase in commercial energy use was slowest. In this group of countries, commercial energy use, on average, increased at the rate of 1.22 per cent per year only. These countries, incidently, are the richest countries of the World and per capita commercial energy use in these countries is already very high. It appears that commercial energy use in these countries is nearing the saturation limit. In addition to high income economies, the rate of increase in commercial energy use during the period under reference has also been found to be relatively slow in lower middle income economies despite the fact that the current levels of commercial energy use in these countries are relatively low.

In contrast to high income and lower middle income economies of the World, increase in commercial energy use has been found to be very rapid in China and India, the two most populous countries of the World. In India, total commercial energy use increased from 0.094 billion metric tones of oil equivalent in 1980 to 0.227 billion metric tones of oil equivalent in 1994. This amounts to an average annual rate of increase of 6.05 per cent per year. In China also, increase in commercial energy use has been found to be quite rapid with an average annual rate of increase of 4.43 per cent per year during the period under reference.

Information about average annual rate of increase in commercial energy use in different countries included in this analysis is given in table 2. Interestingly, this rate has been found to be negative in 21 countries suggesting that total commercial energy use in these countries, instead of increasing, has decreased in 1994 as compared to that in 1980. Out of these 21 countries, 10 countries are classified by the World Bank as low income economies; 7 as lower middle income economies; 3 as upper middle income economies; and 1 as high income economy.

By contrast, in five countries, the average annual rate of increase has been found to be more than 10 per cent per year. These countries are Lithuania, Lebanon, Venezuela, Oman and Singapore. Three of these five countries - Lithuania, Lebanon and Venezuela - are classified as lower middle income economies while Oman is an upper middle income and Singapore is a high income economy. There was no lower income economy where commercial energy use has recorded an average annual rate of increase of more than 10 per cent during the period under reference. The most rapid increase in commercial energy use in the 15 years under reference has been observed in Lithuania where the commercial energy use increased at a whopping average annual rate of increase of more than 17 per cent per year.

In general, the distribution of countries according to average annual rate of increase in total commercial energy use is skewed to the left with majority of the countries in all economies recording a relatively modest rate of increase and a few countries recording an exceptionally high rate of increase in commercial energy use.

Trends and Patterns in Per Capita Commercial Energy Use
A weighted average of per capita commercial energy use in 118 countries of the World included in this analysis suggests that per capita commercial energy use in the World increased from around 1576 kilograms of oil equivalent in 1980 to around 1691 kilograms of oil equivalent in 1994. This means that the per capita commercial energy use in the World increased by about 7 per cent over a period of 15 years or the per capita commercial energy use in the 118 countries of the World increased at an average annual rate of increase of 0.47 per cent per year during the 25 years between 1980 and 1994. This rate of increase, expectedly, has not been same in all countries of the World. It has been highest in the upper middle income economies and slowest in the high income economies.

Inter-country variations from the global average commercial energy use across different economies of the World are substantial in terms of both magnitude as well as in terms of the rate of increase over time. Moreover, these variations have persisted over time. There has been, in fact, very little change in the scenario over time. In high income economies, the average per capita commercial energy use in 1980 was 4711 kilogram of oil equivalent in contrast to a per capita commercial energy use of just 58 kilogram of oil equivalent in the low income economies. This means that per capita commercial energy use in the richest countries of the World was, on average, more than 80 times the per capita commercial energy use in the poorest countries. Over time, there has been only a small reduction in this gap.

Like the different economies, the per capita energy use also varied widely across the countries included in this analysis. The distribution of countries according to the level of per capita commercial energy use is given in table 4. Extreme poverty in terms of per capita commercial energy use in the least developed countries of the World along with the extreme affluence in the most developed countries of the World is very much evident from the table.

During the 15 years between 1980 and 1994, the per capita commercial energy use in the World increased, on average by 115 kg of oil equivalent, ranging from an increase of just 10 kg of oil equivalent in the poorest countries to an increase of 409 kg of oil equivalent in the richest countries. This amounts to an average annual rate of increase of 0.47 per cent per year. The rate of increase has been slowest in lower middle income economies where the commercial energy use increased at an average annual rate of increase of just 0.17 per cent per year - followed by high income economies. By contrast, the rate of increase in per capita commercial energy use has been very rapid in China and India. In India, the per capita commercial energy used increased at an average annual rate of more than 4 per cent per year during the period under reference while in China, per capita commercial energy use, during this period, increased at an average annual rate of more than 3 per cent per year.

The distribution of countries included in this analysis by average annual rate of increase in per capita commercial energy use between 1980 and 1994 is given in table 5. In 21 countries of the World, per capita commercial energy use, instead of increasing has decreased over time. In the remaining countries, in general, the average annual rate of increase in commercial energy use has either been slow or moderate. There are only a few countries in the World where the increase in the per capita commercial energy use has been rapid to very rapid. This shows that there is a general trend of slowing down of the per capita commercial energy use in the World irrespective of the prevailing levels of use.

Distribution of Total Commercial Energy Use
An understanding about the distribution of commercial energy use over a set of geopolitical units can be achieved through a consideration of its components. Distribution of commercial energy use over geopolitical units has essentially two components - extensiveness and intensiveness. The extensiveness of a geopolitical area is nothing but the size of its population relative to other geopolitical areas. On the other hand, the intensiveness of commercial energy use is nothing but the average commercial energy use per person in a geopolitical unit.

A very simple measure of the extensiveness of the distribution of commercial energy use in any geopolitical area is the proportion of population in the area relative to other geopolitical areas. The logic is simple, the more is the population, the more will be the use of commercial energy even if the per capita use remains unchanged. Thus, the proportion of the population of any country to total population of all the countries of the sample may serve as a simple but a useful indicator of the relative extensiveness of the distribution of commercial energy use. If E_s denotes the measure of extensiveness of distribution of commercial energy use, then, it is clear that

$$E_s = P_s / P = p_s$$

where P_s is the population of country s and P is the total population of all countries of the sample.

On the other hand, the intensiveness of commercial energy use may be measured in terms of concentration of commercial energy use. Usually, this concentration is measured in terms of per capita commercial energy use. However, a more refined measure of intensiveness of commercial energy use may be defined by using proportions rather than absolute numbers. Thus, an index of intensiveness of the distribution of commercial energy use in country s, I_s, may be defined as

$$I_s = \text{Log} (c_s / p_s)$$

Where c_s is the proportion of commercial energy use in country s to total commercial energy use in all countries in the sample and Log stands for logarithm to the base 10.

Population and Development: The Indian Perspective

Combining the measure of extensiveness and intensiveness, an index of distribution of commercial energy use for country s, D_s, may be defined as

$$D_s = E_s * I_s$$

Summing over all countries in a region, we get an index of distribution of commercial energy use, D_R, for the region R

$$D_R = \sum D_s = \sum E_s * I_s$$

The logic of the index D should be clear. The second term on the right is essentially a surrogate for per capita commercial energy use. Per capita commercial energy use or any derivative of it is an intensive property and, like pressure, it exists at the level of the individual or the region. But it does not tell about the extent over which this density prevails. As such, it requires a weighing factor to tell for how many people, given intensity prevails. This weighing is done by the index of extensiveness.

It may be noted that the index of extensiveness of commercial energy use is always positive and less than one as it is the ratio of the population of a country to the total population of all countries combined. On the other hand, the index of intensiveness can take both positive as well as negative values. This index is zero when the proportion of commercial energy use in a country is equal to the proportion of population in that country. The index is negative when the proportion of population in a country is greater than the proportion of commercial energy use in that country and vice versa. A positive value of this index is an indicator of the concentration of commercial energy use in that country while a negative value of the index indicates an emptiness in commercial energy use in relation to other countries. Thus if the proportion of commercial energy use and proportion of population is the same in all countries, the index of intensiveness as well as the index of distribution will be zero for the World as a whole. In this way, the index of distribution of commercial energy use and the index of intensiveness also serve as a measure of the relative equality or inequality in commercial energy use across countries. Arguing in a similar manner, the index of the distribution of commercial energy use which is the product of index of extensiveness and index of intensiveness may be conceived as an indicator of the relative equality or inequality in total commercial energy use.

The indices of distribution of commercial energy use along with the indexes of intensiveness of commercial energy use and indexes of extensiveness of commercial energy use for different economies of the World are given in table 6 separately for the years 1980 and 1994. The table clearly shows a very highly unequal distribution of commercial energy use across different economies of the World. Interestingly, the index of distribution of commercial use as well as the index of intensiveness of commercial energy use is positive only in the high income economies. In rest of the economies, the index of distribution of commercial energy use has been found to be negative. This shows that there is concentration of commercial energy use in high income economies whereas in other economies of the World, there is emptiness in the use of commercial energy.

Table 6 also reveals a direct relationship between the level of income and the distribution of commercial energy use. The index of distribution of commercial energy use is lowest in the poorest and least developed countries and as the level of income increase, the index of distribution also increases and becomes highest for the most developed countries of the World. Clearly, the commercial energy use appears to vary with the level of social and economic development and the level of income.

The distribution of the countries included in this analysis according to the level of the index of commercial energy use are given in table 7. Among the 47 least developed countries included in the analysis, there is only one country - Azarbezan - where the index of distribution of commercial energy use has been found to be positive in both 1980 as well as in 1994, although the index has decreased over time. This means that in all but one of the poorest countries of the World, there is gross deficiency in commercial energy use in relation to the population. By contrast, in the richest countries, there were only 3 countries in 1980 where the index of distribution was negative while in 1994, in no country classified as high income economies, the index of distribution was negative. This shows that despite the fact that commercial energy use is increasing rather rapidly in other countries, it continues to be concentrated, very heavily, in the richest countries of the World.

A review of the trend in the index of distribution of commercial energy use in the individual countries included in the sample suggests that in 39 of the 47 poorest countries of the World included in this analysis, the index of distribution of commercial energy use has shown a declining trend in between 1980 and 1994. The remaining 8 countries, characterized as low income economies, where the index of distribution of commercial energy use has increased between 1980 and 1994, are Armenia, Bangladesh, China, Congo, Ethiopia, India, Nepal and Pakistan. Interestingly, five of these eight countries are in Asia and out of these five, four are in South Asia.

In other economies, on the other hand, there appears no clear trend regarding the change in the index of commercial energy use. In the middle as well as in high income economies, the index of distribution of commercial energy has decreased in some countries but increased in others in between 1980 and 1994. In all, there are 45 countries included in this analysis where the index of distribution of commercial energy use has increased during the period under reference indicating an increased concentration of commercial energy use in this countries. Clearly, there appears little relationship between the increase or decrease in the index of distribution of commercial energy use and the level of commercial energy use across the countries of the World.

It would be interesting to explore the factors behind the increase in the index of distribution of commercial energy use. More specifically, it will be interesting to find out whether, the increase in the index of distribution of commercial energy use has been due to the increase in the index of intensiveness or due to the increase in the index of extensiveness or due to the increase in both the indices. The results of our analysis are given in table 8. In 28 of the 45 countries where the index of distribution of commercial energy use has increased between 1980 and 1994, the increase has been due to the increase in the index of intensiveness while in only 5 countries, this increase was due to the increase in the index of extensiveness. Lastly, in 12 countries, both the index of intensiveness and the index of extensiveness have contributed toward increasing the index of distribution of commercial energy use and 8 of these 12 countries are high income economies. In these countries, even a marginal increase in the population appears to result in substantial increase in commercial energy use because of very high per capita commercial energy use.

Conclusions

There has been some substantial increase in the use of commercial energy in the 118 countries included in this analysis during the 15 years between 1980 and 1994 according to the information provided by the World Bank. Most of this increase has been confined to the developed countries of the World. But because of a rapid increase in both population as well as in per capita commercial energy use, the rate of increase in commercial energy consumption in the developing countries of the World has been well above the rate of increase in the developed countries although the level of commercial energy use per capita in these countries remain well below the level of commercial energy use per capita in the developed countries.

Over the years, there has been little change in the scenario related to the use of commercial energy in the World. The richest countries of the World continue to be the main consumers of the commercial energy and the per capita use in these countries has increased even further. On the other hand, the relative contribution of the poorest countries of the World excluding China and India to total commercial energy use in the World has decreased. As the result, the gap between the poorest and the richest in terms of commercial energy use per capita has increased.

What are the implications of commercial energy consumption patterns to development and environment issue that the World faces today? On the basis of the current trends and pattern, one may expect a very rapid increase in the use of commercial energy use in the years to come. This expectation is based on the relationship between the intensiveness of commercial energy use and the level of income. The relationship of intensiveness of commercial energy use with the level of income has been found to be direct - the more is the level of income the higher is the intensiveness of commercial energy use. Though the rate of increase in the intensiveness of commercial energy use appears to have slowed down in recent years yet the rate of increase conceals the real situation as it is affected by what is called the level effect. The reality is that the developed or the rich countries of the World have been the major user of the commercial energy in the past and there is every possibility that these countries shall continue to be the major consumers in future also mainly because the intensiveness of commercial energy use in these countries is very high as compared to other countries of the World.

The implications of the increase in intensiveness of commercial energy use in middle income countries and in China and India are even more serious because these countries have a very large population base which results in a high degree of the extensiveness of commercial energy use. If this trend persists there will undoubtedly be a very rapid shoot up in the commercial energy use in the World in the coming years. There is every possibility of such a shoot up because in the existing development approach, commercial energy use levels are taken as the yardstick for development.

One may therefore expect that the pursuance of the goal of social and economic progress will lead to increase in commercial energy use in all parts of the World. If the poor, developing countries of the World try to achieve the consumption levels of the rich, developed countries as has been the tendency so far, then there will be unbelievable increase in the commercial energy use in the coming years. On the other hand, even if the present status - quo is maintained, the increase in the intensiveness as well as the extensiveness of commercial energy use will still lead to some substantial increase in the use of commercial energy in the coming years.

But what will be implications of this increase in commercial energy use to the sustainability of the environment on the planet Earth? Already signs of environmental decay are visible on the global scenario. Much of this decay is because of the increase in commercial energy use. Any further increase in commercial energy use will put severe pressure on the environment in terms of both resource depletion and wastes generation unless new technology for the generation and for the use of commercial energy is evolved. This means that if the existing development approach is perused, not only an increase in the magnitude of environment problems is expected but the complexities of these problems will also expected to increase further. Obviously these problems are related more to the increase in the intensiveness of commercial energy use. The role of increase in human numbers in the increase in commercial energy use is only secondary to the role of increase in per capita commercial energy use. It is the per capita consumption of energy that matters most. The only way out to deal with the environmental problems, therefore, is to curb the tendency to consume. Though this tendency to consume more and more is the very basis of the existing approach to economic growth and material advancement yet there is no other alternative to save the environment from ultimate collapse than the limiting of the patterns of consumption, particularly of commercial energy.

References

United Nations (1993) Expert Group Meeting on Population Environment and Development. *Population Bulletin of the United Nations*, 34/35: 19-34.

World Bank (1997) *World Development Report, 1997*. Washington, D.C. The World Bank

Table 1:   Use of Commercial Energy in the World.

Economies	Total commercial energy use (Billion metric tones of oil equivalent)		Proportion distribution (Per cent)		Average annual rate of increase (Per cent)
	1980	1994	1980	1990	
LIE	0.073	0.117	1.40	1.70	3.20
India	0.094	0.227	1.80	3.29	6.05
China	0.413	0.791	7.93	11.48	4.43
LMIE	0.492	0.648	9.44	9.40	1.85
UMIE	0.404	0.630	7.75	9.14	3.01
HIE	3.736	4.480	71.68	65.00	1.22
World	5.212	6.892	100.00	100.00	1.88

Table 2: Average Annual Rate of Increase in Commercial Energy Use in the World.

Rate of increase	LIE	LMIE	UMIE	HIE	All
< 0.0	10	7	3	1	21
0.0-2.0	16	3	1	13	33
2.0-4.0	10	8	7	4	29
4.0-6.0	5	4	1	3	13
6.0-8.0	4	4	1	3	12
8.0-10.0	2	1	1	1	5
>= 10.0	0	3	1	1	5

Table 3: Per Capita Commercial Energy Use in the World

Economies	Per capita commercial energy use (Kg of oil equivalent)		Change in per capita commercial energy use		Rate of increase (Per cent)
	1980	1994	Absolute	Proportion	
LIE	58	68	10	17.24	1.02
India	137	248	111	81.02	4.04
China	421	664	243	57.72	3.08
LMIE	929	953	24	2.58	0.17
UMIE	1275	1515	240	18.82	1.16
HIE	4711	5120	409	8.68	0.56
World	1576	1691	115	7.30	0.47

Table 4: Distribution of Per Capita Commercial Energy Use.

Level	Year	LIE	LMIE	UMIE	HIE	All
< 50	1980	16				16
	1994	19				19
50-100	1980	11				11
	1994	9				9
100-250	1980	12	5	1		18
	1994	10	2			12
250-500	1980	5	8	3		16
	1994	6	9	1		16
500-750	1980		7	1		8
	1994	1	4	3		8
750-1000	1980		2	5		7
	1994		4			4
1000-2000	1980	2	2	5	4	13
	1994	1	4	4	1	10
2000-3000	1980	1	3	3	6	13
	1994	1	4	4	5	14
>=3000	1980		3	2	16	21
	1994		3	4	20	27

Population and Development: The Indian Perspective

Table 5:   Distribution of countries according to the rate of increase in per capita commercial energy use.

Rate of increase	LIE	LMIE	UMIE	HIE	All
< 0.0	10	7	3	1	21
1.0-2.0	16	3	1	13	33
2.0-4.0	10	8	7	4	29
4.0-6.0	5	4	1	3	13
6.0-8.0	4	4	1	3	12
8.0-10.0	2	1	1	1	5
>= 10.0		3	1	1	5

Table 6:   Distribution of Commercial Energy Use in the World.

Economies	Index of intensiveness		Index of extensiveness		Index of distribution	
	1980	1994	1980	1994	1980	1994
LIE	-1.434	-1.398	0.380	0.424	-0.544	-0.593
INDIA	-1.061	-0.834	0.207	0.224	-0.220	-0.187
CHINA	-0.573	-0.406	0.297	0.292	-0.170	-0.119
LMIE	-0.229	-0.249	0.160	0.167	-0.037	-0.042
UMIE	-0.092	-0.048	0.096	0.102	-0.009	-0.005
HIE	0.475	0.481	0.240	0.215	0.114	0.103

Table 7:   Distribution of countries according to the index
of distribution of commercial energy use.

Index (10^{-3})	Year	LIE	LMIE	UMIE	HIE
< -10	1980	7	1	1	
	1994	7	1	1	
-10 to -7.5	1980		1		
	1994	1	1		
-7.5 to -5	1980	2	1		
	1994	3			
-5 to -2.5	1980	3			
	1994	4	1		
-2.5 to 0	1980	13	3		3
	1994	15	3		
0 to 2.5	1980	21	18	8	16
	1994	16	16	6	18
2.5 to 5	1980	1	6	6	1
	1994	1	7	8	3
>= 5	1980				6
	1994		1		5

Table 8: Factors behind increase in the index of distribution of commercial energy use.

Economies	Increase in the index of intensiveness	Increase in the index of extensiveness	Increase in both the indices
LIE	5		3
LMIE	13	2	1
UMIE	6	3	
HIE	4		8

Population and Development: The Indian Perspective

An Essay on Population and Consumption as they Affect Environment

Introduction

It is two centuries now when English clergyman Thomas Robert Malthus concluded in his famous essay on population that ultimately there would be only misery and vice in the world because of the simple fact that population would outgrow the subsistence needed to sustain it (Malthus, 1798). Despite the fact that in the 200 years after Malthus, the World is still not caught up in the Malthusian trap, the basic philosophy of Malthus essays has not died down and has flared up again and again in one or the other forms thanks to the socioeconomic and political changes that have taken place from time to time. Recently, there has been a near resurgence of Malthusian thinking in a much broader context which has put in the background the very fact that, till to date, the World has been able to evade the Malthusian trap. Whether the World will be able to evade this dreaded trap in future too, is, basically, the subject matter of this essay.

Focus on the relationship between population and resources needed for its sustenance, in fact, was not confined to Malthusian philosophy alone during the ancient days. Well before Malthus, in 1588, Giovanni Batero suggested that human population did not grow because the environmental resources were insufficient to support larger populations (Batero, 1589). Similar views were also endorsed by Sir Walter Raleigh in 1650 in analysing population growth in Spain (Smith, 1966). The view prevalent during the period was that the size of the population depended primarily on resources available to sustain it.

But with the increase in population, resource availability also increased, mainly because of technological advancement at different times in different places of the World. This technological advancement initiated a chain: more production → more income → more consumption → more resource needs → more waste generation and so on. This chain has threatened the very ecological balance of planet Earth and this very threat has given birth to a new type of trap which asserts that high population growth is a major threat to Earth's environment and hence to the survival of mankind. Incidently, this new thinking has many issues which are similar to Malthusian thinking and, therefore, has been nicknamed as neo-Malthusian thinking.

Despite the fact that the past experience, so far, has negated the above conservative thinking, in many countries of the World, environment is seriously constrained in both ways - resources generation and wastes absorption. This has given credence to the neo-Malthusian thinking that continued high population growth will impinge some major pressures on environment resulting in its depletion to such a level that will endanger the existence of mankind itself. In this paper we attempt to explore the relative role of population and consumption as they influence the environment through an analysis of information on consumption and population growth.

Man and Environment
The relationship between the man and the environment is bidirectional in nature. Environment provides resources to man which the man uses by transforming them into usable form. In this process of transformation of natural resources into usable forms, wastes are generated. These wastes are then absorbed back by the environment. Thus environment serves as both resource base as well as repository of wastes. Maintenance of an environment which makes life possible on Earth, therefore, is the key to the survival of mankind.

The resources that are available to man from environment are in two forms - organic and inorganic. Most of the organic resources are renewable by some natural process going on in the nature while non organic resources are primarily non-renewable. Of late, man has tried to estimate the quantum of organic and inorganic resources on earth. This estimation exercise has indicated that the resource base on earth is limited and this conclusion, in turn, has given a fresh support to Malthusian theory.

Since the resources which are available in the environment are not in a usable form for man, he transforms these resources into usable form through the application of the technology.

Generally, this transformation is not cent per cent efficient and so wastes are generated. These wastes are absorbed, in turn, by the environment. This transformation of natural resources into usable form is known as consumption in the common parlance. Thus, resource needs and the quantum of waste generated depend upon the pattern and level of consumption.

An important issue here is that the capacity of the environment to absorb wastes generated is limited. Excessive wastes generation - as a result of population growth or otherwise - may lead to worsening of the environment. These days, more emphasis is being laid on this aspect of man and environment relationship.

We can now describe the neo-Malthusian trap in more specific terms. Essentially, this conjecture suggests that increased population will require increased resources and, in turn, will generate an increased quantum of wastes. Since the capacity of environment in either generating resources or absorbing wastes is limited, this conjecture fears that, sooner or later, environment will not be able to sustain itself because of the population pressure and will succumb. Since life on Earth is not possible without environment, the extreme of this conjecture is that life on Earth is doomed to death. This conclusion is even more polemic than what Malthus conjectured almost 200 years ago. But we all know that Malthus conjecture has not been proved till today.

We have seen that the basic link between man and environment is through the transformation of resources in the usable form and through the generation of wastes. Both resource needs and wastes generation are affected by population size and consumption patterns. In the next section, we discuss, in some detail, the nature of the World environmental problems.

The Nature of Environmental Problems
The environmental problems that the World is facing today may be classified into two categories. First category of these problems is primarily linked with the man's attempt to control environment. Most of these attempts, success and failure notwithstanding, are only at local - small at global scale - level. They are, basically, outcomes of a mismatch of local environment conditions and the human efforts to generate resources from the environment. They involve those parts of the environment which directly serve the man's interest as, for example, agriculture lands, rivers and in shore ocean waters and land areas containing fuel or minerals deposits. Basically, all these attempts to control environment are associated with one common concern - to ensure continued or even increasing supply of resources for man's need.

A number of effects of these efforts of the man to control environment have been described or suggested. They include desertification, soil erosion, salinisation and water logging, deforestation, etc. It has been hypothesized that these effects will manifest in future both in terms of gravity as well as magnitude because man's attempt to control environment is expected to be more assertive in the days to come. But the evidence for most of these effects are anecdotal and impressionistic. Statistical data on a global scale are merely non statistical generalisation of what is experienced in a small, some times, very small area. Moreover, despite all talks of possible devastating effects of population growth in future, it is difficult, with the currently available evidence, to demonstrate the relationship of these problems with population growth.

One of the few clear-cut examples of the environmental effects of population growth is related with the availability of food. It has been widely hypothesized that an increase in the area of agricultural land to meet out increased food needs of growing population is the main cause of the depletion of forest resources. In fact, arable area in the World increased from 572 millions of hectares to 1414 millions of hectares in the 120 years between 1860 and 1978. It has been estimated that about 7.6 per cent of forests, 7.9 per cent of woodlands, 6.1 per cent of savannas, 10 per cent of grassland and 7.7 per cent of swamps were converted to agriculture land during this period (Revelle, 1984). But, the rate of forest degradation appears to have slowed down despite the fact that population continues to increase (Food and Agricultural Organization, 1980). In fact, for the World as a whole, and for all of its regions except Oceania, the 'population elasticity' of the arable land has decreased considerably during the last 120 years indicating that population growth, alone, may not be the cause of forest depletion. Actually, as may be seen from table 1, the population and arable land relationship for the World as a whole as well as in Europe and Asia has become almost inelastic. The same is true for Canada and USA also. This indicates, that the problem of deforestation etc. may not be linked essentially with the growth of population, especially in the developing countries, through the increasing food needs. The increase in food needs have been met primarily by productivity of agricultural produce and not by an increase in land under cultivation. At present, world food production is increasing by about 2.5 per cent per year whereas the area of cultivated land is growing by only 0.3 per cent.

It may therefore be concluded that the environmental vulnerabilities in the form of deterioration of forests, grasslands etc. which are limited to local level may not be attributed to population growth alone. They may also arise due to inappropriate maintenance and replacement practices. This may be particularly important in poor countries of the World which do not have both technology and means to solve these problems. This leads to question of addressing poverty and underdevelopment. There are conflicting views. One school of thought suggests that poverty is the obvious outcome of rapid population growth. The other professes that poverty leads to high population growth. This line of thinking emphasizes the need of addressing poverty first and stresses that 'development is the best contraception'. If this is so then one of the categories of the environmental problems discussed above should be looked through the unequal distribution of resources in the World, which is primarily responsible for poverty and underdevelopment to many and affluence to a few.

There is another category of environmental problems which have become evident in recent years. These problems are large-scale global problems and their effects are also global. These problems have particularly been responsible for giving a new life to the Malthusian perspective in neo-Malthusian form. These problems, basically, are the results of wastes generated in the transformation of resources into usable forms, and patterns of consumption of resources.

The extent of wastes generated in the process of transformation of natural resources into usable form is primarily a question of technology as well as the type of resources used. It may be pointed out here that the wastes generated through the transformation of organic natural resources are absorbed more readily by the environment as compared to wastes generated in the transformation of inorganic natural resources. Unfortunately, it is extremely difficult to get the idea about the proportion of wastes generated by the transformation of organic and inorganic natural resources for human use. However it is a simple straightforward observation that inorganic resources require more efforts in putting them into usable forms as compared to organic resources. Therefore, the quantum of wastes generated in transforming inorganic natural resources is more than that of organic natural resources.

Let us elaborate this point further by taking the example of transition in agriculture system. Less than 200 years ago, a typical farm family produced its own food, fuel, shelter, draft animals, feed, seeds, tools and implements, and even most of the clothing. Some 80 per cent of the labour force was actually engaged in farm production. Agriculture, at that time was the net energy saver. It had to produce, at least, enough net energy to fuel the agriculturist and his family, even if no excess was required for non farm activities. Today, the situation has changed all together. Agriculture production, today, has become a very complex process. It does not depend on rains and natural fertility of soil like it used to depend in the past. It requires irrigation, fertilizers and pesticides. It also needs transport and storage and many more. The result is that the whole process of food availability - from field to kitchen, and preparation for the table, seems to have reached the point where input of energy into the food production process is greater than the total outcome of the produce that is usable to man. In fact in the so-called more developed countries of the World, food production process has become a net energy looser.

One may think of the famous law of thermodynamics in this context. In the present reference, this law may be described through the following equation:

$$\text{Resource} + \text{Energy} \xrightarrow[\text{Process}]{\text{Transformation}} \text{Production} + \text{Wastes}$$

This equation simply states that total inputs and total outputs in any production system are the same. The problem today is that the use of energy in the transformation process has increased substantially because of the use of non organic resources as an input into the process.

The second issue related with wastes generation is the consumption pattern. More consumption, obviously, leads to more wastes generation. But the increase in consumption may be due to both an increase in population as well as an increase in per capita consumption as a natural corollary of the current development trend which advocates maximization in every facet of life. In discussing population and environment relationship, therefore, it is imperative that the relative contribution of the increase in population and relative contribution of per capita increase in consumption is analysed in detail. It is in this context that we focus on the World consumption patterns in the next section.

Consumption Patterns

The needs of the earliest man were minimal - just to secure food for survival. For thousands of years, man subsisted on raw food available from the environment. Subsequently, he discovered fire and started cooking the raw food. With time, he learnt so many things like shelter, clothing, agriculture etc. However, comparative to the period of man's presence on Earth, up till very recently, the man's basic needs were confined primarily to food, cloth and shelter, and a large share of man's efforts was devoted to securing these basic needs. Those were the days when both utilisation of resources as well as the generation of wastes were linked closely to man's capacity to work. In this period, man subsisted primarily on organic substances simply because it was much easier to transform the organic substances into usable form.

However, the machine revolution in Europe in the 18th century opened up new avenues to the man for the transformation of resources into usable form. The introduction of machines ensured, for the first time, that this process of transforming resources into usable forms was free from the limitations of human effort. This change, commonly known as technological change, altered the consumption pattern all together. Since the 18th century, the rapid advancement in technology has provided the man almost unlimited means to transform the available natural resources into usable form. More, importantly the process has not stopped yet and almost routinely man is inventing techniques and methods through which more and more resources can be put at man's disposal.

This increase in the use of resources, combined with some very substantial population growth of the World during past two centuries has put severe stresses on the environment. Results of these stresses on the ecosystem are already apparent in the form of greenhouse effect, deforestation and resources depletion etc. It has been feared in this context that if these stresses are not checked, the eco-balance will collapse leading to the extinction of life on Earth. Supporters of this view have the empirical evidence in their favour. If we limit our discussion to commercial energy consumption, alone, then between 1980 and 1994, total commercial energy use in the World increased from 5.212 billion metric tonnes in 1980 to 6.892 billion metric tones in 1994. There is every possibility that with continued efforts for social and economic development, this consumption will increase further and that too, at a much faster rate. Clearly, the neo-Malthusian theory has some truth in highlighting the consequences of rapid population growth.

But increase in the use of resources is not confined to increase in population only. An important factor in the increase in the use of resources has been some very substantial increase in per capita resources utilization throughout the World. This increase in per capita resources use has no relationship with the rate of population growth. In fact, total resources utilization in any country is the product of per capita resources used and the size of the population. If R denotes the total resources use, C the per capita resources used and P the size of the population, then

$$R = C * P \qquad (1)$$

The above relationship can be used to analyse the relative role of increase in per capita resources use and the increase in the size of the population to total increase in resources used. If R_1, C_1 and P_1 denote respectively the total resources used, per capita resources used and size of the population at the earlier date and R_2, C_2 and P_2 denote the same at a later date, then it can be shown that

$$R_2 - R_1 = (C_2-C_1)* (P_1+P_2)/2 + (P_2-P_1)*(C_1 +C_2)/2 \quad (2)$$

The first term on the right of equation (2) represents the contribution of the increase in per capita resources use to the increase in total resources use. Similarly, the second term represents the contribution of increase in the size of the population. In this way, application of the equation (2) permits to analyse the relative role of increase in per capita commercial energy use and increase in population in the increase in total energy use.

We have applied the above approach to analyse the relative role of increase in per capita commercial energy use and increase in population to the increase in total commercial energy use between 1980 and 1994 in 118 countries of the World for which data are made available by the World Bank (World Bank, 1997). The data maintained by the World Bank suggests that in these countries, total commercial energy use increased from about 5.2 billion metric tones of oil equivalent in 1980 to about 6.9 billion metric tones of oil equivalent in 1994 - an increase of almost 1.7 billion metric tones of oil equivalent over a period of 15 years. During this period, total population of these 118 countries increased from 3.306 billion in 1980 to 4.076 billion in 1994 while the per capita commercial energy use increased from 1576 Kg of oil equivalent in 1980 to 1691 Kg of oil equivalent in 1994. Obviously, both increase in population and increase in per capita commercial energy use have contributed to the total increase in commercial energy use in these countries. However, an application of equation (2) suggests that for the 118 countries taken together, the increase in per capita commercial energy use during the period 1980 through 1994 had contributed for almost 52 per cent of the total increase in the commercial energy use. By contrast, increase in population appears to have contributed for about 48 per cent of the total increase in commercial energy use during the above period.

An application of equation (2) to different countries of the World, however, reveals a situation which is drastically different from the global average. It may be seen from table 1 that the relative contribution of population growth and increase in per capita commercial energy use varies widely across different economies of the World, a terminology used by the World Bank to classify individual countries. In the countries classified as Lower Middle Income Economies by the World Bank, for example, more than 90 per cent of the increase in commercial energy use during the period 1980-94 has been found to be accounted by the increase in per capita commercial energy use. By contrast, in China, 70 per cent of the total increase in commercial energy use has been accounted by the increase in the size of the population. In Low Income and Upper Income Economies also, as may be seen from table 1, the main contributor to increase in commercial energy use appears to be the increase in per capita use and not the increase in population. On the other hand, in India, like China, it is the growth in the size of the population which appears to be primarily responsible for the increase in total commercial energy use.

The above simple analysis clearly shows that it is not the population alone which is behind all the environment related problems that the World is facing today. It is clear from the analysis that even if the World achieves the goal of zero population growth, there is little chance for any let up in the situation simply because the extent of resources utilization and associated wastes generation will continue to increase as the result of the tendency towards maximization of per capita resources use. Interestingly, this tendency towards maximization of per capita resources use is derived from the basic approach of economic development that has now been universally adopted. Population growth plays no role in the tendency towards maximization of per capita resources consumption.

Maximization of per capita resources utilization has implications for both resources depletion and wastes generation. Incidently, most of the environmental problems which are global in nature are associated with the issue of wastes generation and not the resources depletion. The problems related to the resources depletion are mostly local in nature. The rate of wastes generation depends, rather heavily, on both the consumption level as well as the type of resources needed. At low consumption levels, most of the transformed resources are used to meet out basic necessities of life - food, clothing and shelter. Normally, this consumption has a limit. But when resources are transformed to meet out the luxuries of life - as is usually the case at high consumption level - consumption has no limit. Incidently, the amount of wastes generated in meeting out basic necessities of life is much less than that generated in providing luxuries.

What is even more important is the difference between the type of resources needed to meeting out the basic necessities of life and the type of resources needed in providing luxuries to the life. Resources need for meeting out basic necessities essential for survival are primarily organic in nature while the resources used in providing luxuries to life are inorganic in nature. Organic resources, generally, produce less wastes as compared to their inorganic counterparts when they are transformed into usable form through the application of the technology. Moreover, unlike the inorganic resources, the wastes generated through the transformation of organic resources are, generally, absorbed by the environment itself. A third important point is that many, in fact most, of the organic resources are renewable while inorganic resources are, basically, not renewable. In fact, the pattern of resources utilization that we witness today have been heavily guided by the World economic order. The World economic order, today, is characterized by accumulation of wealth, capital intensive technology and a market based economy which is driven not by the basic necessities of the man but by the market forces. In this order, the basic motto is accumulation of wealth through maximization of production. However, maximization of production is possible only through the maximization of per capita consumption or per capita resources utilization. As such, the prevailing World economic orders contributes, in its own subtle way, towards maximization of per capita resources utilization and hence towards the problems of resources depletion and wastes generation which leads to a decay of the environment. Population growth also has a role to play in this situation as a rapid population growth can result in a significant increase in the resources utilization and associated wastes generation even at low per capita resources utilization levels as has been the experience in China and India. Interestingly, efforts to control the growth of population have been pursued vigorously in the World in the recent past, especially in the developing countries where the growth of population continues to be rapid but little emphasis has been given on modifying the World economic order so as to make it eco-friendly despite the fact that even the achievement of zero population growth will not help in addressing the environment related problems because of the prevailing World economic order.

Conclusions

The fear of environmental degradation in the form of dis-balancing of the ecosystem and depletion of natural resources has primarily been instrumental in the re-emergence of Malthusian perspective in the neo-Malthusian form in recent years. Like Malthus, the proponents of neo-Malthusian perspective believe in positive checks on population to solve World development problems. In order to give credence to their approach, they foresee in population growth, the root of all development ills that the World faces today. It is in this context that they emphasize a cut in population growth through induced efforts in order to achieve a rapid rate of social and economic development.

There are, however, critiques of the above approach. This school of thought opines that it is not the population growth but the World social and economic order which is the root of all problems of the World including the differential population growth and the problems related to the decay of the environment. This school, therefore, professes an alteration in the present World economic order in a way which is more eco-friendly.

The present analysis suggests that both the patterns of per capita resources utilization and the growth in population have contributed in their own way to the situation that prevails in the World today. As such, by simply curtaining the population growth, the problems related to the degradation of the environment cannot be addressed on a permanent basis. It is important that a serious thought is given to the pattern of resources utilization as this pattern also have important implications for environmental degradation in terms of resources depletion and wastes generation. Since, the existing evidence suggests that the population growth rates in throughout the World are slowing down while the per capita resources utilization is showing an increasing trend indicates that, in the years to come, it is the trend in the per capita resources utilization and not the rate of increase in population which will determine the nature as well as the magnitude of the environment problems. Since the per capita resources utilization is driven mostly by the prevailing economic order, it appears, that population and environment issues should be discussed and debated in the context of plenty to a few and scarcity to many.

References

Malthus. T.R. (1798) 1960. *On Population.* New York, Modern Library.

Botero, G (1589) 1956. *The Reason of State.* New Heaven, Yale University Press.

Smith, RL (1966) *Ecology and Field Biology.* New York, Harper and Row.

Revelle, R (1984) The effects of population growth on renewable resources. In United Nations *Population Environment and Development*. New York, United Nations.

Food and Agricultural Organization (1980) *FAO Production Yearbook*. Rome, FAO.

Table 1: 'Population elasticity' of arable land in the World: 1860-1978.

Region	Population elasticity	
	1860-1920	1920-1978
Africa	0.44	0.30
Asia	0.51	0.10
Latin America and Caribbean	0.72	0.33
Canada & USA	2.01	-0.02
Europe	0.16	0.01
Oceania	1.57	2.23
USSR	1.24	0.54
World	0.77	0.17

Population and Development: The Indian Perspective

Table 2: Relative contribution of population growth and increase in per capita commercial energy use to the increase in commercial energy use in 118 countries, 1980-1994.

Region	Net increase in energy consumption (Million tones of oil equivalent)	Proportion of increase due to	
		Increase in per capita consumption	Increase in population
Low-income economies	44	0.68	0.32
India	133	0.33	0.67
China	378	0.30	0.70
Lower-middle income economies	156	0.91	0.09
Upper-middle income economies	226	0.61	0.39
High income economies	744	0.54	0.46
Total	1681	0.52	0.48

Population Policy in India

Introduction

The current focus on the relationship between population and development is phrased in sharp contrast to earlier lines of argument. The ruling paradigm in the two decades following the second World War was that if the developing countries of the World adopted a path of rapid economic development based on advanced science and technology based modern manufacturing sector, they would be able to improve the quality of life of their people. But rapid economic growth has been witnessed only rarely in the developing countries (Lipton 1982). There is practically no 'trickle down' effect visible in most of the developing countries. This failure of a development approach based on rapid economic growth in tackling the interconnected problems of disease, hunger and poverty led to thinking in another direction. Among the rampant uncertainties of 1950s, with confidence outrunning data, development experts of the so-called developed countries started propagating a model of social and economic development which was based on a 'target group' approach. This approach had two dimensions - one focussing on improvements in nutrition, medical care, sanitation, income and employment through the provision of skill and productive assets and other on reducing population growth through the establishment of small family norm by educating the people and by providing it with better maternal and child care as well as better contraceptive technologies. Population size, its growth, and its many other characteristics including patterns of migration and urbanization became important components of development policy in this approach.

Since the uncertainties of 1950s, the role of population and related factors in the development process has become more clear and the advocacy of integrating population related factors into development planning process, is now based on a sound base. A number of countries now feel that growth of their population is a deterrent in their efforts to improve the quality of life of the people and have initiated programmes which attempt to reduce the excessive population growth. This thinking about the possible link between population and quality of life and the efforts which try to regulate the size and growth of the population comes under the purview of what is known as the population policy.

India, the second most populous country in the World, was the first country to recognize the role of population related factors in the development process as early as in 1951 when it launched its first Five Year Development Plan. The purpose of this write up is to discuss the evolution of the population policy in the country and the impact of this policy on the size and growth of the population.

Demographic Situation in India around Independence

At the time of Independence, the Indian population was in a pitiful condition. Diseases and hunger were prevalent throughout the country and the expectation of life was very low. During the colonial period there was little attempt to improve the productivity of agriculture to provide food for the masses. Similarly, there were little efforts for the prevention of unwanted morbidity and mortality. The vicious circle of poverty, malnutrition and disease leading to numerous untimely and premature death was at its full swing during this period. Whatever development activity was there, it was oriented towards the colonial rulers and not towards the population at large. Even the minimal health and other facilities that were created during that period, were available to only a small elite section of the community. The population, at large, was devoid of even the basic minimum facilities that lead to improved health status.

From the demographic viewpoint, population of the country at the time of Independence may be characterized as one in which the process of transition was not started at all. In other words, throughout the country, exceptionally high birth rate and exceptionally high death rate as well as infant and child mortality rates prevailed, resulting in a very low expectation of life at birth and a relatively low rate of growth of population as the high birth rate was almost equally compensated by a high death rate. The disease spectrum during that period was dominated by endemic disease like cholera and small pox.

These totally unsatisfactory patterns of mortality, morbidity and fertility were associated with extreme poverty and some very low levels of literacy and age at marriage, particularly for females.

In any case, the population growth rate prior to the Independence was not alarming at all as it was always below 1.5 per cent per year throughout the twentieth century prior to the Independence. However, there were unmistakable signs of a possible mismatch between the levels of birth and death rate in the near future as the death rate was showing a continuously declining trend since 1921 but the birth rate was almost stationary. At the time of the Independence, the death rate was still able to compensate for most of the high birth rate that prevailed in most parts of the country. As the result, the dependency was low because a substantial proportion of all births were not able to see the first birth day and a major proportion of those who survived up to first birth day were unable to see their fifth birth day. It may therefore be concluded that though poverty and hunger were major concerns at the time of Independence, they were certainly not generated by rapid population growth.

Evolution of Population Policy
The evolution of any policy, basically, has two phases. First is the view or perception about the prevailing situation and second is the action taken to alter the situation. It may very well happen that there may not be a match between the perception and action. But perception and action jointly constitute a policy. In analysing any policy evolution, therefore, it is important to discuss separately, the evolution of the perception and the development of action and then to correlate the two. As such,

we first focus upon the perception about population and related issues of our leaders at the time of the Independence. It may be pointed out that when India adopted its population policy, it was a surprise to the many as nowhere in the world, there was a doubt that the rapid economic development would not lead to improvements in the quality of life. The debate on the role of population related factors in the social and economic development was not started at that time in its real sense. As such, an important question is what prompted our leaders to adopt a well-defined population policy and to integrate it in the development planning process. Up to 1951, the growth of Indian population was not alarming at all. Therefore, in order to analyse the factor behind the adoption of a population policy, it is necessary to get an idea about the perception of our leaders at the time of the Independence, particularly Gandhi and Nehru, about the impact of population growth on social and economic development.

Gandhi, in all his writings, was never explicit about a probable population problem. His approach to social and economic development was a philosophical one based on the concepts of social affection, doctrine of non possession, and trusteeship (Divan and Lutz, 1985). He was of the opinion that once the society is developed in its own terms of reference, it would adjust itself and found its own solution about such problems as excessive population growth. As such he was of the view that the need of the time was a new social order and not one or two isolated and narrow in scope interventions.

In comparison to Gandhi, Nehru was less idealistic in transforming the society. He has covered more population related issues in his writings than Gandhi. He was more explicit on the problem of population, particularly falling birth rate in the west, in his 'The Discovery of India' and related it to the concept of national decay. He has mentioned the industrial revolution and spread of modern technology as the reason behind rapid population growth in Europe. But on China and India he is explicit in mentioning that their huge populations are a burden and a weakness unless they are properly and productively organised. He says further that an eastward sweep of modern technology will result in substantial increase in population. But for India, he wanted that the country would be better off with fewer people than a bigger population which may result in because of the eastward sweep of modern technology (Nehru, 1946).

Another factor which appeared to have played a key role in incorporating issues related to integration of population in development planning in India after the Independence was the Great Bengal famine of 1943-44. The official Famine Inquiry Commission reported about 1.5 million deaths which is now regarded as an underestimate by one of the member of the Commission (Aykroyd, 1974). By an account, around 3 million people died in that famine. (Sen, 1981). The Commission, in his report to the British Government stressed the need for population control efforts as an integral part of any development strategy. Similarly, the first Health Survey and Development Committee, popularly known as Bhore's Committee also stressed the adoption of a rational family planning programme (Government of India, 1946).

At the political stage, the women's wing of Indian National Congress also played a major role in putting forward the idea of planned family though not in the context of population growth but in the context of status of woman. At the time of the Independence, the woman's wing of Indian National Congress was very strong with some very popular women like Rajkumari Amrit Kaur, Vijay Laxmi Pandit who played a leading role in India's struggle for freedom. Nehru, who was more inclined to communist ideology and was progressive in thinking than any other political leader at that time, appears to have been influenced by these developments. However, whatever Nehru wrote in his autobiography in the Ahmednagar jail dates back to all these developments, reports and contextual situation. Clearly, Nehru had his own thinking about population which, in the course of time got support from others also, although in different contexts.

When Nehru got the reins of the Government of India after the Independence, he made it sure that steps should be taken to check a possible substantial increase in population of the country in the future as a result of technology invasion as it happened in Europe. He was particularly inclined to socialistic form of development by properly and productively utilizing the existing population. He was very well aware of the fact that an unproductive population was a burden to national interests and national economy. That is why he was of the view that India would be better off with fewer people than a bigger population. This wisdom of Nehru formed the fundamental setting for the adoption of population policy in India as early as in 1952, in the form of a programme for 'family limitation and population control'. It happened to be the first official family planning programme in the World.

The programme for 'family limitation and population control' aimed at a   Assessment of an accurate picture of factors contributing to rapid population growth,

b   Identification of suitable techniques of family planning and devise methods by which knowledge of these techniques could be widely disseminated,

c   Provision of advice on family planning as an integral part of service of government hospitals and public agencies. (Government of India, 1952).

In addition to the above objectives, the Government believed that there already existed some intrinsic demand for family planning and therefore opened family planning clinics. This was the beginning of the clinic-based approach in India's family planning programme.

During the Second Five Year Plan (1956-61), the clinic-based approach of family planning services delivery system gained momentum and a more vigorous action-cum-research oriented programme was undertaken. Family planning services were made available at all hospitals and dispensaries in the country and the number of family planning clinics increased from 147 to 4165. Sterilization operation was included for the first time in the family planning programme. Overall, the Planning Commission of India observed a notable progress in the programme during this period (Government of India, 1960).

But the 1961 census was an eye opener to political leaders and development policy planners in the country. During 1951-61 there was a sudden spurt in population mainly because of considerable reduction in crude death rate whereas the crude birth rate remained almost stationary. The results of the 1961 population census led to a considerable rethinking about how to reduce the abnormally high birth rate and the focus was concentrated on family planning. In the attempt to push the family planning programme, the clinic-based approach was replaced by the extension approach during the Third Five Year Plan (1961-66). Further, realising the importance of the programme in country's social and economic development, Government created a separate Department of Family Planning in the Ministry of Health and Family Planning. For the first time in the history of the programme, the emphasis was placed on time bound and target oriented activities. The document of the Third Five Year Plan stated that "the objective of stabilizing the growth of population over a reasonable period must be at the very centre of planned development. (Government of India, 1971).

The period 1966-69 was a plan holiday for the country. During this period, however, family planning programme was integrated with the public health programme and the delivery of family planning services was extended through the commercial distribution of condoms.

During the Fourth Five Year Plan (1969-74), the National Family Planning Programme was included among the programmes of highest priority in the context of social and economic development and for, the first time a numerical target was set to reduce the birth rate from 39 to 25 per thousand population within a period of ten to twelve years. Sterilization became the major plank in the Government strategy to achieve the targets within the stipulated time frame.

The only other feature of this period was the adoption of the Medical Termination of Pregnancy Act which liberalised the grounds of induced abortion.

By the beginning of the Fifth Five Year Plan (1974-79), it was increasingly realised that the family planning programme achieved only a limited success in curbing the growth of population. The population of the country continued to grow rapidly despite all focus on population control and all efforts to promote family planning at the government level. The results of the 1971 population censes led to a revision of the demographic goals. The new goals called for the reduction of birth rate to 30 by 1979 and to 25 by 1984. These targets were followed by a new population policy adopted by the Government in 1976. Salient features of this policy were:

1.   Raising the minimum age at marriage from 15 to 18 years for girls and from 18 to 21years for boys.

2.   Increase in the amount of monetary compensation for sterilization for both males as well as females.

3.   A freeze in people's representation in Lok Sabha, and State Legislative on the basis of 1971 census up to 2001.

4.   Basing the devolution of taxes and duties and sanction of grant-in-aid on population figures of 1971 until 2001.

5.   Making of 8 per cent of central assistance to State plans on the basis of the performance in family planning.

6.   Introduction of compulsory sterilization and specific measures of incentives and disincentives to family planning.

In a nutshell, the principal thrust of the new population policy was to accelerate efforts to control population through a rigorous implementation of the National Family Planning Programme so as to ensure a rapid decrease in the crude birth rate.

But during the general elections of 1977, there was a political change and the Government who adopted the above population policy was voted out. To many, this political reversal was caused by the anguish and anger showed by the population against harsh, stringent and sometimes even coercive measures adopted for the promotion of family planning, particularly, sterilization. In any case, the new Government went up to the extreme and changed the name of the programme from family planning to family welfare with the pretext that maternal and child health services and nutrition should also be the part of any population control strategy. In the Sixth Five Year Plan, the new Government fixed the target of bringing down the birth rate to 30 per thousand population by around 1982-83 (Government of India, 1983). An operational plan of action was also developed to achieve this target. This plan of action, among other things, outlined the magnitude of the work in terms of number of sterilizations to be done, the IUDs to be inserted and conventional contraceptives to be distributed.

However, the most notable feature of this period from the view point of population policy was a complete reversal of the Government from the concept of compulsion to the concept of voluntarism. It was made very clear that all the family planning activities would have to be promoted purely on the basis of the voluntary approach, with no pressure of any kind on the couples who did not practice family planning despite having many children. Moreover, annual targets for family planning methods under the programme were reduced drastically.

The so-called political sensitivity of population issues in India that first reflected in 1977 general elections has resulted in a somewhat cautious approach towards population related issues, especially at the political level. Since 1977, every statement on population related matters from the Government has emphasized the fact that all the steps and measures proposed to be undertaken were purely voluntary. At the policy level, however, top priority was assigned to the problem of excessive population growth in the thrust towards social and economic development. But the fear of political backlash nearly forced the Government not to opt for stringent measures to achieve population goals. More emphasis was given to the incentives that may attract the couples to accept family planning. Some of these incentives which were introduced at that time do provide some significant benefits in terms of economic gains. However, the social and cultural aspects of population growth, particularly the reproductive behaviour was given only a passing attention in the policy documents. Similarly, the policy also recognized the importance of the integration of population control activities with the other social and economic development activities but how this integration will be achieved at the level of implementation has not been elaborated in any document. The fact is that the policy has been implemented rather vertically which appeared to be one of the reasons for its poor effectiveness.

Trends in population policy in India have been synthesized in table 2. The consistency of the Indian Government about the matters related to population is clear from the table. Another important feature of the policy is the widening of its base over time. Till 1974, population policy in the country covered only the issues of population growth and fertility. Now the policy covers nearly all components of population as well as such factors as age at marriage and spatial distribution.

Like policy, efforts to modify population related variables in the broad context of population policy have also undergone a transition. In the early days of population policy, efforts were concentrated mainly to reduce fertility through increased contraception. Since 1978, the scope of the policy has been widened to include maternal and child health services also. This meant a focus on modifying the mortality situation too. Recently, steps have also been taken to modify the current levels and trends in the spatial distribution of the population. However, National Family Welfare Programme as continues to be the mainstay of population control efforts in the country.

The policy towards population and its control in India underwent a sea change in the Seventh Five Year Plan. On the basis of the recommendations put forward by a Working Group on Population Policy constituted by the Government, the system of allocating the birth rate targets were dispensed away. Rather the issue of population growth was given a broad base by incorporating mortality related concerns in the policy.

Moreover, two types of goals were fixed - the long term goal and the short term or intermediate goals. The long term goal of the population policy was fixed in terms of Net Reproduction Rate. It was targeted that a Net Reproduction Rate of one was to be achieved by the year 2001. On the other hand, the short term or intermediate goals of the policy were related to issues like practice of contraception, female age at marriage, etc. For the first time, the importance of mortality reduction in population control was recognised at the policy level as the long term goal of NRR=1 by 2001 cannot be achieved by reducing fertility alone. Therefore, targets for the reduction of such mortality indicators as crude death rate and infant mortality rate were also specified along with the targets of crude birth rate and total fertility rate under the National Family Welfare Programme. Similarly, intermediate goals in the areas of immunization, and maternal health etc. were also fixed along with the targets for new acceptors of different methods of family planning to be recruited every year. However, the emphasis continued to be on fertility reduction though it was accepted that reduction in fertility was not possible without a parallel reduction in mortality.

Today, Government promotes family planning programme on voluntary basis as a people's movement, in keeping with democratic traditions of the country. The programme seeks to promote responsible parenthood with a two child norm through independent choice of the methods of family planning best suited to acceptor. The programme emphasizes voluntary acceptance of family planning without resort to any form of pressure or coercion (Government of India, 1987). At the beginning, population policy in India may be described as a population influencing policy but since then, the nature of the policy has somewhat changed and currently, it may be regarded as a policy which is guided more by the population responsive approach than by a population influencing approach. Today, reduction in the growth of population in India is regarded by many development experts as a compulsion for achieving rapid social and economic progress. This compulsion, in fact, may be found reflected very explicitly in all Five Year Development Plan documents of the country since Independence. However, because of the political sensitivity that got attached to population issues, the political commitment to the policy has generally been confined to statements and appeals to masses only. Moreover, there is very little attempt, even at the policy level to integrate activities that influence different components of the population policy. At the policy level, the population policy of the Government of India remains very well defined and based on a sound rationale. How, this clear and well defined policy on population in the context of social and economic development has been operationalised is a matter of discussion and debate. Incidentally, it is the efficiency and effectiveness of the implementation process which ultimately determines the success or failure of any development policy or programme.

A synthesis of different versions of the population policy in the country suggests that the policy towards population in India has been very explicit and its origin has been related more to poverty and hunger than growth of population. Moreover, it was a population influencing policy in the beginning as the demographic situation was not the cause of policy evolution at the time of Independence. However, after 1961, the policy has turned more and more population responsive primarily because of some rapid increase in population. In order to implement the policy, very specific measures have been undertaken which, sometimes, have even turned coercive but the political commitment towards the population policy has not been very strong because of the political sensitivity attached to family planning. The final result is that the impact of the policy has not been very strong.

Family Welfare Programme Organization
The programmes to operationalise the goals and the objectives of the population policy can be divided into two categories - programmes related to altering fertility and mortality levels, and programmes related to migration patterns and spatial distribution of population. This distinction is basically based on the nature of the services. The programmes related to fertility and mortality operate at the micro level while the programmes related to migration and spacial distribution are carried out only at the macro level. In any case, both types of programmes merit attention in discussing the population policy.

As mentioned earlier, the population policy in India focussed primarily upon the reduction of birth rate up to 1974. As such the efforts to implement the policy were confined to the reduction of birth rate only. The main tool to reduce the birth rate was the promotion of the practice of contraception for which, the National Family Planning Programme was launched. Initially, the programme focussed primarily upon family limitation rather than family spacing. The result was that over the years, the programme drifted towards the promotion of terminal methods of contraception such as sterilization at the cost of birth spacing methods like intra-uterine devices and oral pills. Even today, the programme depends upon the terminal methods so heavily that it has been nicknamed as the sterilization programme. This relative neglect of spacing methods of contraception has been attributed to dismal impact of the programme by a number of researchers.

As regards mortality, the population policy did not cover mortality related issues in its early years. However, health care development had been undertaken even before the Independence with the constitution of a Health Survey and Development Committee in 1946. This committee, popularly known as Bhore's Committee, gave specific recommendations for the development of health care delivery system in India. After the Independence, several such committees have been formed and suggestions and recommendations put forward by these committees have resulted in the development and expansion of the health and family welfare services delivery infrastructure throughout the country in the form of primary health centres, sub-health centres etc. In 1978, India signed the Alma-Atta Declaration and adopted the goal of "Health for All" through primary health care approach as one of the components of its development strategy. This led to a renewed vigour for the extension of health care delivery system and for the first time efforts were made to involve the community through the recruiting of voluntary health workers and training of traditional birth attendants. An important feature of this time was an effective integration of health and family planning services. The Expanded Programme of Immunization was launched during this phase with the assistance of World Health Organisation to prevent the mortality and morbidity from communicable diseases among children. In 1985, efforts to reduce morbidity and mortality from communicable diseases gained additional momentum when first Universal Immunization Programme and then the Technology Mission on

Immunization was launched in the country. As a result there was substantial reduction in infant and child mortality rate during the eighties as compared to seventies when these rates remained almost stagnant. It may be pointed out here that high infant and child mortality are supposed to be major deterrent in regulating fertility behaviour under the framework of what is known as the "Child Survival Hypothesis".

Efforts to modify fertility, however, continue to be focussed upon the promotion of family planning practices, particularly sterilization. Recently there has been a lot of discussion on the promotion of spacing methods but the programme continues to be centred round the sterilization. There have been efforts to raising the legal minimum age at marriage and to legalizing abortion at least in a restricted sense but all these efforts could not be effective at the implementation level because of the traditional and orthodox nature of the society. The impact of all these interventions on fertility levels has been found to be, at best, minimal.

Recently, the Government has evolved the reproductive and child health approach to address population related issues. This approach integrates all activities related to promotion of contraception, safe motherhood and child survival into a coherent, unified framework for implementation. Another important feature of the approach is that the practice of allocating targets for the recruitment of new family planning acceptors under the National Family Welfare Programme has been abolished. The new approach calls for assessing the needs of the community as regards family planning and plan and organize activities and programmes to fulfil these needs. The new approach also emphasizes upon the health related problems of women especially reproductive tract infections and sexually transmitted diseases in an attempt to widen the base for family planning services.

Coming to the programmes and interventions related to migration and spatial distribution, population policy in India regards the migration in and out of the country as satisfactory. On the other hand concern about spatial distribution was mentioned in the policy for the first time in 1976 only. This reflection about spatial distribution in the policy documents, however, was preceded by a need for exploring the potentialities of developing small and medium towns in the country which was highlighted during the Fourth Five Year Plan Document. Though, this issue was mentioned as one of the objectives of the Fifth Five Year Plan, yet it was only during the Sixth Five Year Plan that a scheme of integrated development of small and medium towns was introduced by the Government. But for a number of reasons, most important of which was the lack of appropriate information and suitable planning, the scheme could not make much headway. In fact, there is little spatial planning in the country. There is only some physical planning at the urban settlement level which is totally inadequate to meet the needs of objectives and goals outlined in population policy. There is a total lack of regional or sub-regional spatial plans which are essential to put the objective of the population policy regarding spatial distribution into actual implementation. At the same time little efforts have so far been made to develop and implement a comprehensive plan for modifying spatial patterns of population. This is so despite the fact that there has been very rapid urban population growth in the country in recent years.

Achievements of the Population Policy

Information available from the programme service statistics permits a discussion on the achievements of the population policy at the national level. However, the programme service statistics is known for errors of duplication over time, place and method. Despite these errors, the time series of programme service statistics makes it possible to have some idea about the achievements of population policy in the country.

Family planning achievements, under the National Family Welfare Programme may be termed as both satisfactory as well as unsatisfactory. As on 31 March 1995, more than 45 per cent of the married couples were effectively protected against conception. Over the years, the programme has been able to expand itself and has established particularly in the rural areas of the country.

However, the signs of unsatisfactory performance of the programme are more than those which may be exampled. As mentioned earlier the programme continues to depend heavily upon sterilization which has resulted in a high mean age of acceptors. The fertility impact of the programme, therefore, is not as much as it should be. Moreover, there are very little signs of improvement in the quality of services available through the programme, despite vast expansion of the services delivery system and huge investment into it.

Another disheartening feature of the programme is the persistence of regional disparities in its performance. In the Central India, comprising of the States of Uttar Pradesh, Bihar, Rajasthan and Orissa which account for a major share of the country's population, the performance of the programme continues to be poor. In Utter Pradesh, Bihar and Rajasthan, proportion of couples effectively protected are below 40 per cent against the national average of 45 per cent.

Not only, the achievements of the programme vary among the States of the country, but there are wide variations in the efficiency and administrative capacity of the programme itself. An analysis of regional variations in the efficiency of the programme has revealed that the programme has failed to adapt itself to the changing needs of the community and has developed a somewhat rigid, stagnant structure (Chaurasia, 1989). This analysis has also concluded that significant improvements in the programme performance may be achieved only if the programme is able to improve its own organisational efficiency and administrative capacity.

Findings of the analysis are supported by the difficulty faced by programme administrators in shifting the programme emphasis from sterilization to spacing methods in order to widen its base. Because of its rigid structure and typical form of management and administration which gives low importance to community based paramedical staff as compared to a medical graduate posted at the family welfare centres, the programme has not been successful to adapt itself to changing needs of the people.

Impact of the Population Policy
The Indian approach to population in the context of social and economic development has been a subject of intensive scrutiny throughout the World. At least two reasons may be cited for this interest. First one, obviously, is the very fact that the Indian family planning programme was the first ever such programme launched in any part of the World. The other reason was the

challenge of Indian demography, as the population of the country is the second largest in the World. An equally important factor has also been the availability of information on India. Information about the other population giant - China, it may be pointed out - has been available only recently.

Expectedly, all the studies on the impact of population policy have been confined to the evaluation of the family planning programme in terms of its contribution in lowering the birth rate. Programmes to modify mortality situation and spatial distribution have not been the subject of such intensive scrutiny as the programme of promoting family planning practices. Reasons are many but the most important of all these is the fact that it is the high birth rate which is primarily responsible for the high rate of population growth.

Evaluation of family planning programme, in turn, can be divided into two categories. First category is related to the measurement of the number of births averted as the result of acceptance of family planning methods being promoted in the context of the implementation of the population policy. Such an evaluation has been carried out routinely by the administration of the National Family Welfare Programme on the basis of programme service statistics (Government of India, 1995). In another direction, births averted due to the practice of family planning methods have been estimated on the basis of survey based estimates of family planning practices in India by applying the contraceptive prevalence model (Chaurasia 1989a). The contraceptive prevalence model, it may be pointed out, is the latest techniques available for measuring the impact of family planning practices (Bongaarts, 1985).

Table 9 gives the information on the total number of births averted as the result of the use of different methods of family planning being promoted under the National Family Welfare Programme in the country during the period 1970 through 1995. These estimates have been arrived at on the basis of an estimation technique developed by the administration of the National Family Welfare Programme and are based on the programme service statistics that are generated routinely through the inbuilt monitoring and reporting system of the Programme. The point that is important here is that these estimates do not take into consideration the prevalence of contraception outside the programme.

According to the estimates prepared on the basis of the official programme services statistics, by the year 1994-95, more than 182.76 million births had been averted in the country as the result of the practice of different family planning methods. It is however, clear that most of these births averted were due to sterilization. The contribution of other methods such as intra-uterine device, oral pills and condoms to the total births averted has remained almost marginal.

Conclusions
Many reasons may be cited for the limited impact of population policy in India. From the programme side, the policy has been sound but it's implementation has not been up to the mark. Many potential ideas have been wasted due to over exploitation, while others have been under utilized. There has been a tendency among the programme administrators to search for ideal solutions. This tendency has resulted in a practice of polarization drifting from one solution to another - but none offered a complete remedy.

The experience and research, however, suggest that the variables endogenous to the population policy and programme can have a marked impact on population growth. A combination of innovative approaches with an efficient services delivery system can do the miracle. The need is to tone up the administrative capacity and organisational efficiency of the programme so that it can meet the ever changing needs of the population by providing an efficient services delivery system.

In the end, it is not difficult to conclude in an equivocal note. The pursuance of a well defined population policy in India has definitely achieved a lot but a lot more is still more to be achieved. Opportunities for a more broadly conceived population programme are immense. It is the responsibility of the polity of the country to translate their commitment, as reflected in the policy documents, into urgent and top priority action.

References

Aykroyd, W.R.(1974) *The Conquest of Famine.* London: Chicago.

Bongaarts J(1985) Contraceptive Prevalence Model. In United Nations, *Methods to Enhance Evaluation of Family Planning Programmes.* New York, United Nations.

Chaurasia A.R.(1989) *Analysis of Demographic impact of family welfare programme in India.* Datia, Shyam Institute.

Chaurasia, A.R.(1989a) *Regional Variations in the efficiency of family welfare programme in India*. Datia, Shyam Institute.

Divvan R and Lutz M (1985) *Essays in Gandhian Economics*. New Delhi, Gandhi Peace Foundation.

Government of India (1952) *First Five Year Plan*. New Delhi, Planning Commission.

Government of India (1960) *The Second Five Year Plan, Progress Report 1959-60*. New Delhi, Planning Commission.

Government of India (1971) *The Third Five Year Plan 1961-66*. New Delhi, Planning Commission.

Government of India (1983) *Draft Five Year Plan 1978-83*. New Delhi, Planning Commission.

Government of India (1996) *Yearbook of Family Welfare Programme in India*. New Delhi, Ministry of Health and Family Welfare.

Nehru, Jawaharlal (1946) *The Discovery of India.*

Sen, A. (1981) *Poverty and Famines*. London : Oxford University Press.

United Nations (1989) *Trends in Population Policy*. New York, United Nations.

Table 1: Selected Population Related Indicators in India at the Time of the Adoption of Population Policy.

Indicator	1941		1951
Population size (million)	318.7		361.08
Average annual growth rate		1.26	
Birth rate		39.90	
Death rate		27.40	
Life expectancy		32.50	
Index of aging	12.8		15.07
Young dependency	67.28		65.96
Old dependency	8.62		9.94
Overall dependency	75.90		75.90
Median age of population	21.00		21.10
Singulate age at marriage (M)		19.93	
(F)		15.43	
Children born surviving up to age 20 (M)		57.9	
(F)		58.6	
Literacy among population with age 10 years and more	15.1		
Enrolment ratio based on population aged 5-24	12.6		

Table 2:   Trends in Population Policy in India.

Variable	1974	1983	1993
Population growth			
View Policy	Too high Lower	Too high Lower	Too high Lower
Fertility			
View Policy	Too high Lower	Too high Lower	Too high Lower
Contraceptive use			
Policy	No limits Direct support	No limits Direct support	No limits Direct support
Limits to access	No limits	No limits	No limits
Mortality			
View Policy	High Reduce	High Reduce	High Reduce
Immigration			
Quantum View Policy	Not significant Satisfactory Maintain	Not significant Satisfactory Maintain	Not significant Satisfactory Maintain
Emigration			
View Policy	Not significant Satisfactory Maintain	Not significant Satisfactory Maintain	Not significant Satisfactory Maintain
Spatial distribution			
View Policy	Inappropriate Decelerate	Inappropriate Decelerate	Inappropriate Decelerate

Table 3: Desired Demographic Goals in India Under Various Plans

Year	Specified demographic goal	Target year
1962	CBR = 25	1973
1966	CBR = 25	As expeditiously as possible
1968	CBR = 23	1978-79
1969	CBR = 32	1974-79
1974	CBR = 30	1979
1976	CBR = 30	1978-79
1977	CBR = 30	1978-79
1978	CBR = 30	1982-83
1980	NRR = 1 CBR = 29 CBR = 21 CDR = 10.4 = 9 IMR = 90 < 60 CPR = 36.6 = 42.0 = 60.0 Universal immunization of children Antenatal care = 70 per cent	By 2001[*] By 1990 By 2001[*] By 1990 By 2001 By 1990 By 2001 By 1985 By 1990 By 2001 By 2001 By 2001

Table 4:   A synthesis of Population Policy in India.

Key issues	Status
Nature of the policy	Explicit
Nature of the policy	Initially influencing but now more and more responsive.
Origin	More related to poverty and hunger than to population factors.
Political commitment	Not very strong because of the political sensitiveness attached to the programme.
Measures taken	Very specific. Some times coercive in the past. Now purely voluntary in nature.
Impact	Not very effective in checking population growth.

Table 5:   Salient Features of Family Planning Programme in India

1.	Delivery points		
	a.	Rural Family Welfare Centres (1986)	5435
	b.	Primary Health Centres (1996)	21853
	c.	Community Health Centres (1996)	2424
	d.	Sub Health Centres (1996)	132727
	e.	Urban Family Welfare Centres (1994)	1291
2.	Manpower in Rural FW Centres		
	a.	Doctors (1996)	26930
	b.	Block Extension Educator	5621
	c.	LHV	18904
	d.	ANM	133773
3.	Traditional birth attendants trained as on 1.4.96		660996
4.	Village health guides trained		320360
5.	Expenditure on family welfare (million Rs)		
	1974-75		686
	1980-81		1409
	1986-87		5688
	1993-94		13126

Table 6: New acceptors recruited under Family Welfare Programme in India (In thousand).

Year	Sterilization	IUD	Condom	Oral Pill	Total
1970-71	1330	476	1963		3769
1973-74	942	372	3010		4324
1976-77	8261	581	3634	58	12534
1979-80	1778	635	2987	82	5482
1982-83	3983	1097	5765	183	11028
1985-86	4902	3274	9387	1358	18920
1988-89	4678	4851	12422	2416	24368
1991-92	4090	4386	13875	3366	25717
1994-95	4580	6702	17707	4873	33862

Table 7:   Contraceptives Method Mix in India.

Year	Couples currently and effectively protected			
	All methods	Sterilization	IUD	Others
1970-71	100	77	13	10
1973-74	100	83	7	10
1976-77	100	88	4	8
1979-80	100	89	4	7
1982-83	100	85	5	10
1985-86	100	76	11	13
1988-89	100	64	13	13
1991-92	100	62	13	14
1994-95	100	58	14	16

Table 8:   Couples effectively protected.

Year	Proportion of couples effectively protected (Per cent)			
	Sterilization	IUD	Others	All Methods
1970-71	8.0	1.4	1.0	10.4
1973-74	12.2	1.0	1.5	14.7
1976-77	20.7	1.1	1.7	23.5
1979-80	19.9	1.0	1.4	22.3
1982-83	22.0	1.4	2.5	25.9
1985-86	26.5	3.7	4.7	34.9
1988-89	29.8	5.9	6.2	41.9
1991-92	30.3	6.7	7.2	44.1
1994-95	30.2	7.2	8.5	45.8

Table 9:   Births averted due to National Family Welfare
              Programme in India.

Year	Number of births averted (million)			
	Sterilization	IUD	Others	Total
1970-71	1.40	0.33	0.19	1.92
1973-74	2.44	0.26	0.30	2.99
1976-77	3.07	0.24	0.41	3.72
1979-80	4.29	0.22	0.40	4.91
1982-83	4.59	0.30	0.59	5.47
1985-86	5.97	0.83	1.31	8.12
1988-89	7.47	1.56	1.85	10.87
1991-92	8.19	2.08	2.43	12.70
1994-95	8.63	2.35	3.03	14.01

Population Transition in India: 1950-2050

Introduction

It is well known that, in any closed population, net addition to it in a given period is equal to the difference between the number of births and number of deaths in that period. If in a given period, number of births in a population are equal to the number of deaths, i.e. if the ratio of number of births to number of deaths is one, then there is zero population growth. Denoting by B, the number of births and by D the number of deaths in a population in a given period, this means that population will not increase in the given period if $B/D = 1$; it will increase if $B/D > 1$; and decrease if $B/D < 1$. Clearly, more the ratio B/D deviates from the value 1, the more rapid will be the increase or decrease in population. This means that the ratio B/D can be used as an indicator to analyse population transition over a given period of time in any population.

If B_1 and D_1 denote total number of births and deaths respectively at the beginning of the period t and B_2 and D_2 at the end of the period then the average annual rate of change in the ratio births to deaths over the period t is given by

$$
\begin{aligned}
r\,(\,B/D\,) \quad &= (1/t)\ln\,[(B_2/D_2)/(B_1/D_1)] \\
&= (1/t)\ln\,[(B_2/B_1)/(D_2/D_1)] \\
&= (1/t)\,[\ln(B_2/B_1) - \ln(D_2/D_1)] \\
&= r(B) - r(D) \quad\quad\quad (1)
\end{aligned}
$$

This means that the rate of change in the ratio of births to deaths in any population is equal to the algebraic difference between the rate of change in the total number of births and rate of change in total number of deaths respectively. Now

$$
\begin{aligned}
B \quad &= N * CBR \\
&= N * TFR * (CBR/TFR) \\
&= N * TFR * ASB \quad\quad\quad (2)
\end{aligned}
$$

where N represents population size, TFR is the total fertility rate and $ASB = CBR/TFR$ measures the age structure effects on the crude birth rate (Horiuchi, 1991). In other words

$$
r(B) = r(N) + r(f) + r(bf) \quad\quad\quad (3)
$$

where $r(N)$ is the rate of change in population size, $r(f)$ is the rate of change in total fertility rate and $r(bf)$ is the rate of change in the age structure effects on the crude birth rate. Thus the rate of change in the total number of births in any population in a given period is nothing but the algebraic sum of the rate of change in population, rate of change in total fertility

156

rate and the rate of change in the age structure effects on the crude birth rate. Arguing in a similar manner, it can easily be shown that

$$D = N * LDR * (CDR / LDR)$$
$$= N * LDR * ASD \qquad (4)$$

where LDR is the life table death rate and ASD = CDR/LDR, like ASB, is the age structure effects on crude death rate. Hence

$$r(D) = r(N) + r(l) + r(dl) \qquad (5)$$

where r(l) is the rate of change in LDR and r(dl) is the rate of change in the age structure effects on the crude death rate.

Substituting from (3) and (5) in (1), we get

$$r(B/D) = r(f) - r(l) + r(bf) - r(dl) \qquad (6)$$

Equation (6) suggests that the rate of change in the ratio of total number of births to total number of deaths r(B/D) in a given period may be decomposed into four factors: 1) rate of change in the levels of fertility as measured by total fertility rate; 2) rate of change in the levels of mortality as measured by life table death rate; 3) rate of change in the age structure effects on the crude birth rate; and 4) rate of change in the age structure effects on the crude death rate.

It is also clear from equation (6) that the rate of change in the ratio of births to deaths essentially has two components - the level component and the age structure component. The level component of population transition is represented by the difference [r(f) - r(l)]. Total fertility rate and life table death rate are synthetic measures of fertility and mortality respectively. They are defined over a hypothetical population. They measure the chance of a birth and chance of a death respectively in any population independent of age structure effects. The difference [r(f) - r(l)], therefore, is an indicator of the increase in population net of population age structure. Similarly, the second component [r(bf)-r(dl)] may be viewed as the effect of changes in the age structure of population on population transition through changes in the age structure effects on the crude birth rate and the crude death rate. Thus, transition in any closed population is dependent upon the differential rate of change in the probability of a birth and the probability of a death and on the differential growth rate in the age structure effects on the crude birth rate and the crude death rate. Equation (6) permits us to measure the relative contribution of change in the levels of fertility and mortality as well as change in the age structure effects on crude birth rate and crude death rate on population transition.

The above considerations suggest that the index $I = r(B/D)$ may be used as an indicator for measuring population transition in any closed population. It can be used over a period of time in the same population as well as across populations over the same period. In the first situation, an analysis of the trend in the index $I = r(B/D)$ can give the idea about population transition and relative contribution of changes in the levels of fertility and mortality as well as changes in the age structure effects on the crude birth rate and the crude death rate to the observed transition; the larger the value of $r(B/D)$ during any period, the slower will be the transition in population during that period and vice versa. In the second case, a comparison of r(B/D) and its components for two or more populations for the same period of time may be used to compare the pace of transition in the populations under consideration and the reasons for the difference in the pace of transition.

Application to India

We have applied the above methodology to study the past trends and future prospects of population transition in India. Data for the analysis has been taken from United Nations Data Bank which maintains information on population and related demographic indicators for its member countries. Estimates prepared by the United Nations are revised at every two years. In the present analysis, 1994 revision of estimates of population size and vital rates are used (United Nations, 1995). Estimates of vital rates are for five year period while the estimates of population size are available for single years in the United Nations Data Bank.

Estimates of population size, crude birth rate, crude death rate, total fertility rate and expectation of life at birth for India for the period 1950 through 2050 are given in table 1. Information up to the year 1990 are estimates while information beyond 1990 are projections. United Nations prepares four variants of population projection - medium, high, low and constant fertility change. The four projections differ in terms of assumptions about trends in fertility only. Mortality trends in all the four projections are the same. In this analysis, only the first three variants of projection have been used. Projection and related estimates of vital rates based on the assumption of constant fertility change are not used in this analysis.

Population and Development: The Indian Perspective

According to the information available from the United Nations Data Bank, the population of the country, in 1950, was estimated to be 357.561 million which increased to 850.638 million by the year 1990. This population is expected to reach between 1.35 to 1.98 billion by the year 2050 depending upon the nature of fertility transition in the years to come. Under the low variant of projection which assumes a very rapid fertility decline, the population of the country is expected to reach 1.35 billion by the year 2050. On the other hand, if fertility continues to decline at a slow pace, the high variant of projection suggests that the population of the country will shoot up to 1.98 billion. In the most likely scenario of fertility decline adopting a middle course, the medium variant of the projection exercise suggests that the population of the country will reach somewhere near to 1.64 billion by the year 2050. This means that in the next 60 years, the population of the country is likely to be doubled from the population in the year 1990 under the most likely scenario of medium variant projection.

The above stated growth in the population of the country is largely the result of prevailing levels of fertility and mortality and the age structure effects on the crude birth rate and the crude death rate. During the period 1950-55, the country had a crude birth rate of 44.1 and a crude death rate of 25.0 per 1000 population. These rates decreased to 31.3 and 11.2 per 1000 population respectively by the period 1985-90. By the period 2045-50, the crude birth rate is expected to decrease to 13.4 per 1000 population in case of medium variant projection; to 17.5 in case of high variant projection; and to 9.3 in case of low variant projection. The decline in the crude death rate, however, varies with the type of projection. In case of medium variant, the crude death rate is expected to reach the lowest level of 6.9

per 1000 population by the period 2015-20 and then is expected to increase due to aging of the population so as to reach 9.1 deaths per 1000 population by the year 2050. In case of high variant, the crude death rate is expected to reach the lowest level of 6.8 by the period 2020-25 and then is expected to increase to 7.9 by the year 2050. Similarly, in case of low variant projection, the crude death rate is expected to reach the lowest level of 7 death per 1000 population during the period 2015-2020. Beyond the year 2020, the crude death rate is expected to increase so as to reach a level of 10.7 deaths per 1000 population by the year 2050.

As the result of the above trends in the crude birth rate and the crude death rate in the country, the ratio of total births to total deaths is expected to start decreasing only after the period 1995-2000. This ratio was only 1.7640 during the period 1950-55 but it increased to 2.7946 by the period 1985-90. Under the medium variant projection, this ratio is expected to reach a maximum of 2.9888 by the period 1995-2000. Beyond 1995-2000, the ratio is expected to start decreasing, reaching a level of 1.4725 by the period 2045-50. By contrast, under the high variant projection, this ratio is expected to reach an all time high of 3.1867 during the period 2005-10 and is expected to decline to 2.2152 by the period 2045-50. Finally, in case of low variant projections, this ratio is expected to start decreasing after 1995 to reach 0.8692 by the period 2045-2050. This implies that there appears little possibility of achieving zero population growth in the country at least up to the year 2045. It is only after 2045, that the population of the country will stop increasing.

In table 3, the rate of change in the ratio of births to deaths, r(B/D) has been presented along with the difference between the rate of change in total fertility rate and the rate of change life table death rate [r(f)-r(l)] and the difference between the age structure effects on birth rate and the age structure effects on the death rate [r(bf)-r(dl)]. It may be seen from the table that the rate of change in the ratio of births to deaths in the country, although positive, has decreased continuously during the period 1950-55 through 1975-80. This implies that though the ratio of births to deaths has increased, yet this increase has gradually slowed down. However, during the period 1975-80 through 1980-85, the rate of change in births to deaths increased indicating that the slowing down of the increase in the ratio of births to deaths has been reverted during this period. Main reason for this reversal was the slow down in fertility decline.

Average annual rate of change in total number of births in the country decreased rather rapidly during 1950-55/1975-80 from 1.91 per cent to 0.24 only. But during the period 1975-80/1980-85, there had been a very substantial increase in total number of births in the country. As the result the average annual rate of change in the total number of births increased to 1.61. Between 1980-85 to 1985-90.

In terms of population transition, the above trends imply that the pace of population transition in the country increased continuously up to the period 1975-80 but during the period 1975-80 through 1985-90, it slowed down considerably. This period, incidently, was the most turbulent period for the population control efforts. It is characterized by a very strong political commitment and resulting pressure and even coercion and force for promoting family planning during the days of

162

Emergency and a near total lack of initiative and drive in the post Emergency period.

The role played by the age structure effects on the crude birth rate and the crude death rate in population transition is clear from table 3. Since 1965-70, increase in the ratio of births to deaths can be attributed to the differing age structure effects on crude birth rate and crude death rate. It may also be seen from the table that the difference [r(bf)-r(dl)] has increased up to the period 1980-85 which suggests that changes in the age structure of the population has been an important factor in slowing down population transition in the country. Although, the rate of change in [r(bf)-r(dl)] has started decreasing after 1980-85, yet this difference will continue to be positive up to the period 2015-20 in all the three projection scenarios. This means that by the period 2015-20, the age structure effects on crude birth rate and crude death rate would continue to slow down transition in population of the country.

Decomposing the rate of change in the ratio of births to deaths to its level component and age structure component suggests that the period 1950-55 to 2045-50 can be divided in to four sub-periods. During the period 1950-55 through 1970-75, both the level component as well as the age structure component have contributed in the same direction to the rate of change in the ratio of births to deaths. On the other hand, during the period 1975-80 through 1985-90, a positive rate of change in the ratio of births to deaths had been largely due to a positive difference [r(f)-r(l)]; the difference [r(bf)-r(dl)] being negative throughout this period. In case of medium variant population projection, this situation is likely to persist up to the end of this century. Beyond the year 2000 and up to the year 2020, the negative rate of change in the ratio of births to deaths is expected to be largely due to a negative value of the difference [r(f)-r(l)] which is expected to overcome the positive value of the difference [r(bf)-r(dl)]. It is also clear that during the period 1995-2000 through 2015-20, the rate of change in the age structure effects on crude birth rate and crude death rate component is expected to slow down transition in population as measured by the ratio of total births to total deaths. Lastly, during the period 2015-20 through 2045-50, the difference [r(f)-r(l)] is expected to turn positive again but this positive difference is expected to be overcome by the negative value of the difference [r(bf)-r(dl)]. During this period, the prevailing levels of fertility and mortality are expected to slow down transition in population whereas the age structure effects on crude birth rate and crude death rate are expected to hasten it.

In case of high and low variants of population projection also, the situation remains more or less the same with some minor shifts in the time when negative value of the difference [r(f)-r(l)] overcomes the positive value of the difference [r(bf)-r(dl)]. In case of high variant population projection, the negative value of the difference [r(f)-r(l)] is expected to overtake the positive value of the difference [r(bf)-r(dl)] only during the period 2005-10/2010-15 whereas in case of low variant of projection, this overtaking is expected to occur during the period 1990-95/1995-2000. Thus, the ratio of total births to total births in the high variant projection is expected to start declining 10 years later than that in the medium variant projection. On the other hand, in case of low variant, this ratio is expected to start decline 10 years earlier.

Conclusions

The analysis presented here highlights the fact that the past population transition in India has been and the future transition is expected to be a complex combination of the rate of change in the level of fertility and mortality and the rate of change in the age structure effects on crude birth rate and crude death rate. On the basis of the population projections prepared by the United Nations, it may be concluded that in the immediate future, the rate of change in the age structure effects on crude birth rate and crude death rate will be such that it will slow down the pace of population transition in the country as determined by the rate of change in total fertility rate and life table death rate. In the current population scenario, it is only after 2020 that the rate of change in the age structure effects on crude birth rate and crude birth rate is expected to contribute towards accelerating the pace of population transition in the country. Age structure effects on crude birth rate and crude death rate may be regarded as medium-term trend which are attributable to change in the age structure of the population as the result of decline in the levels of fertility and mortality. With the decline in the levels of fertility, the proportion of population who are young decreases leading to an increase in the proportion of population in other age groups, including the childbearing ages. This results in an increase in the total number of births even at low fertility levels. Similarly, the decrease in the number of persons in the younger age groups results in a decrease in the total number of deaths. The net result, therefore is that the ratio of births to deaths increases despite a reduction in the levels of both fertility and mortality.

References

Horiuchi S (1991) Measurement and analysis of cohort size variations. *Population Bulletin of the United Nations*, 30: 106-124.

United Nations (1995) *World Population Prospects, 1994.* New York, United Nations.

Table 1: Estimates and projection of population and selected demographic indicators in India: 1950 - 2050.

Year	Population	CBR	CDR	TFR	E(0)	LDR
ESTIMATES						
1950	357561					
1955	395096	44.1	25.0	5.97	38.7	25.84
1960	442344	43.6	21.7	5.92	42.6	23.47
1965	495157	42.0	19.4	5.81	45.4	22.03
1970	554911	40.2	17.5	5.69	48.0	20.83
1975	620701	38.2	15.8	5.43	50.3	19.88
1980	688856	34.7	13.9	4.83	52.9	18.90
1985	768185	33.8	12.6	4.47	55.4	18.05
1990	850638	31.3	11.2	4.07	57.9	17.27
MEDIUM VARIANT PROJECTION						
1995	935744	29.1	10.0	3.75	60.4	16.56
2000	1022021	26.6	8.9	3.42	62.8	15.92
2005	1107222	24.1	8.1	3.09	65.0	15.38
2010	1189082	21.7	7.4	2.76	67.2	14.88
2015	1263691	19.3	7.1	2.43	68.9	14.51
2020	1327110	16.7	6.9	2.10	70.5	14.18
2025	1392086	16.6	7.1	2.10	71.8	13.93
2030	1455086	16.2	7.3	2.10	72.9	13.72
2035	1513315	15.5	7.7	2.10	74.0	13.51
2040	1563604	14.7	8.1	2.10	74.9	13.35
2045	1605232	13.9	8.6	2.10	75.8	13.19
2050	1639863	13.4	9.1	2.10	76.6	13.05

Year	Population	CBR	CDR	TFR	E(0)	LDR
HIGH VARIANT PROJECTION						
1995	938422	29.7	10.0	3.83	60.4	16.56
2000	1030545	27.8	9.0	3.58	62.8	15.92
2005	1125460	25.8	8.2	3.34	65.0	15.38
2010	1221662	23.9	7.5	3.09	67.2	14.88
2015	1316123	22.0	7.1	2.85	68.9	14.51
2020	1406100	20.1	6.9	2.60	70.5	14.18
2025	1501507	20.0	6.8	2.60	71.8	13.93
2030	1599465	19.6	7.0	2.60	72.9	13.72
2035	1697721	19.1	7.2	2.60	74.0	13.51
2040	1793609	18.4	7.4	2.60	74.9	13.35
2045	1887086	17.8	7.6	2.60	75.8	13.19
2050	1979932	17.5	7.9	2.60	76.6	13.05
LOW VARIANT PROJECTION						
1995	933037	28.5	9.9	3.66	60.4	16.56
2000	1013445	25.4	8.9	3.25	62.8	15.92
2005	1088967	22.4	8.0	2.84	65.0	15.38
2010	1156641	19.5	7.4	2.42	67.2	14.88
2015	1211811	16.4	7.1	2.01	68.9	14.51
2020	1249722	13.2	7.0	1.60	70.5	14.18
2025	1286318	13.1	7.3	1.60	71.8	13.93
2030	1317890	12.6	7.8	1.60	72.9	13.72
2035	1341559	11.9	8.3	1.60	74.0	13.51
2040	1354211	10.9	9.0	1.60	74.9	13.35
2045	1355113	9.9	9.8	1.60	75.8	13.19
2050	1345936	9.3	10.7	1.60	76.6	13.05

Table 2: Average annual number of births and deaths in India.

Period	Births	Deaths	B/D
ESTIMATES			
1950-55	16596087	9408213	1.7640
1955-60	18256192	9086224	2.0092
1960-65	19687521	9093760	2.1649
1965-70	21106367	9188095	2.2971
1970-75	22454189	9287335	2.4177
1975-80	22720814	9101421	2.4964
1980-85	24623993	9179358	2.6825
1985-90	25334580	9065409	2.7946
MEDIUM VARIANT PROJECTION			
1990-95	25991858	8931910	2.9100
1995-2000	26038275	8712054	2.9888
2000-05	25657378	8623434	2.9753
2005-10	24914898	8496325	2.9324
2010-15	23669259	8707344	2.7183
2015-20	21633188	8938263	2.4203
2020-25	22569327	9653146	2.3380
2025-30	23062093	10392178	2.2192
2030-35	23005108	11428344	2.0130
2035-40	22615355	12461522	1.8148
2040-45	22023410	13625995	1.6163
2045-50	21742137	14765182	1.4725
HIGH VARIANT PROJECTION			
1990-95	26567541	8945300	2.9700

Period	Births	Deaths	B/D
1995-2000	27368641	8860352	3.0889
2000-05	27812465	8839621	3.1463
2005-10	28048108	8801708	3.1867
2010-15	27915635	9009137	3.0986
2015-20	27358341	9391669	2.9130
2020-25	29076070	9885864	2.9412
2025-30	30389526	10853402	2.8000
2030-35	31488126	11869870	2.6528
2035-40	32120236	12917921	2.4865
2040-45	32758186	13986641	2.3421
2045-50	33836408	15274721	2.2152
LOW VARIANT PROJECTION			
1990-95	25417369	8829191	2.8788
1995-2000	24720321	8661845	2.8539
2000-05	23547014	8409648	2.8000
2005-10	21894678	8308750	2.6351
2010-15	19421306	8408005	2.3099
2015-20	16246118	8615366	1.8857
2020-25	16611062	9256546	1.7945
2025-30	16406510	10156411	1.6154
2030-35	15823722	11036713	1.4337
2035-40	14691947	12130965	1.2111
2040-45	13411154	13275688	1.0102
2045-50	12559878	14450612	0.8692

Table 3:   Rate of change in the ratio of total number of births and deaths and their components.

Period	r(B/D)	r(f)-r(l)	r(bf)-r(dl)
ESTIMATES			
1950-55/1955-60	0.0260	0.0175	0.0085
1955-60/1960-65	0.0149	0.0090	0.0060
1960-65/1965-70	0.0119	0.0070	0.0049
1965-70/1970-75	0.0102	0.0000	0.0102
1970-75/1975-80	0.0064	-0.0133	0.0197
1975-80/1980-85	0.0144	-0.0063	0.0206
1980-85/1985-90	0.0082	-0.0099	0.0181
MEDIUM VARIANT PROJECTION			
1985-90/1990-95	0.0081	-0.0079	0.0160
1990-95/1995-2000	0.0053	-0.0106	0.0160
1995-2000/2000-05	-0.0009	-0.0134	0.0125
2000-05/2005-10	-0.0029	-0.0159	0.0130
2005-10/2010-15	-0.0152	-0.0205	0.0053
2010-15/2015-20	-0.0232	-0.0246	0.0014
2015-20/2020-25	-0.0069	0.0037	-0.0106
2020-25/2025-30	-0.0104	0.0030	-0.0135
2025-30/2030-35	-0.0195	0.0030	-0.0225
2030-35/2035-40	-0.0207	0.0024	-0.0231
2035-40/2040-45	-0.0232	0.0024	-0.0256
2040-45/2045-50	-0.0186	0.0021	-0.0207
HIGH VARIANT PROJECTION			
1985-90/1990-95	0.0122	-0.0037	0.0159
1990-95/1995-2000	0.0079	-0.0057	0.0136
1995-2000/2000-05	0.0037	-0.0070	0.0107

Period	r(B/D)	r(f)-r(l)	r(bf)-r(dl)
2000-05/2005-10	0.0025	-0.0089	0.0115
2005-10/2010-15	-0.0056	-0.0112	0.0056
2010-15/2015-20	-0.0124	-0.0138	0.0014
2015-20/2020-25	0.0019	0.0037	-0.0017
2020-25/2025-30	-0.0098	0.0030	-0.0129
2025-30/2030-35	-0.0108	0.0030	-0.0138
2030-35/2035-40	-0.0129	0.0024	-0.0154
2035-40/2040-45	-0.0120	0.0024	-0.0144
2040-45/2045-50	-0.0111	0.0021	-0.0132
LOW VARIANT PROJECTION			
1985-90/1990-95	0.0059	-0.0128	0.0187
1990-95/1995-2000	-0.0017	-0.0160	0.0142
1995-2000/2000-05	-0.0038	-0.0201	0.0163
2000-05/2005-10	-0.0121	-0.0254	0.0132
2005-10/2010-15	-0.0264	-0.0321	0.0058
2010-15/2015-20	-0.0406	-0.0410	0.0005
2015-20/2020-25	-0.0099	0.0037	-0.0136
2020-25/2025-30	-0.0210	0.0030	-0.0241
2025-30/2030-35	-0.0239	0.0030	-0.0269
2030-35/2035-40	-0.0337	0.0024	-0.0362
2035-40/2040-45	-0.0363	0.0024	-0.0387
2040-45/2045-50	-0.0301	0.0021	-0.0322

Table 4: Rate of change in crude birth rate, total fertility rate, crude death rate, life table death rate and age structure effects on crude birth rate and crude death rate.

Period	r(b)	r(f)	r(bf)	r(d)	r(l)	r(dl)
ESTIMATES						
1950-55/1955-60	-0.0023	-0.0017	-0.0006	-0.0283	-0.0192	-0.0091
1955-60/1960-65	-0.0075	-0.0038	-0.0037	-0.0224	-0.0127	-0.0097
1960-65/1965-70	-0.0088	-0.0042	-0.0046	-0.0206	-0.0111	-0.0095
1965-70/1970-75	-0.0102	-0.0094	-0.0009	-0.0204	-0.0094	-0.0111
1970-75/1975-80	-0.0192	-0.0234	0.0042	-0.0256	-0.0101	-0.0155
1975-80/1980-85	-0.0053	-0.0155	0.0102	-0.0196	-0.0092	-0.0104
1980-85/1985-90	-0.0154	-0.0187	0.0034	-0.0236	-0.0088	-0.0147
1985-90/1990-95	-0.0146	-0.0164	0.0018	-0.0227	-0.0085	-0.0142
MEDIUM VARIANT PROJECTION						
1990-95/1995-2000	-0.0180	-0.0184	0.0005	-0.0233	-0.0078	-0.0155
1995-2000/2000-05	-0.0197	-0.0203	0.0006	-0.0188	-0.0069	-0.0120
2000-05/2005-10	-0.0210	-0.0226	0.0016	-0.0181	-0.0067	-0.0114
2005-10/2010-15	-0.0234	-0.0255	0.0020	-0.0083	-0.0050	-0.0033
2010-15/2015-20	-0.0289	-0.0292	0.0003	-0.0057	-0.0046	-0.0011
2015-20/2020-25	-0.0012	0.0000	-0.0012	0.0057	-0.0037	0.0094
2020-25/2025-30	-0.0049	0.0000	-0.0049	0.0056	-0.0030	0.0086
2025-30/2030-35	-0.0088	0.0000	-0.0088	0.0107	-0.0030	0.0137
2030-35/2035-40	-0.0106	0.0000	-0.0106	0.0101	-0.0024	0.0125
2035-40/2040-45	-0.0112	0.0000	-0.0112	0.0120	-0.0024	0.0144
2040-45/2045-50	-0.0073	0.0000	-0.0073	0.0113	-0.0021	0.0134
HIGH VARIANT PROJECTION						
1990-95/1995-2000	-0.0132	-0.0135	0.0003	-0.0211	-0.0078	-0.0133
1995-2000/2000-05	-0.0149	-0.0139	-0.0011	-0.0186	-0.0069	-0.0117
2000-05/2005-10	-0.0153	-0.0156	0.0003	-0.0178	-0.0067	-0.0112
2005-10/2010-15	-0.0166	-0.0162	-0.0004	-0.0110	-0.0050	-0.0060
2010-15/2015-20	-0.0181	-0.0184	0.0003	-0.0057	-0.0046	-0.0011
2015-20/2020-25	-0.0010	0.0000	-0.0010	-0.0029	-0.0037	0.0007
2020-25/2025-30	-0.0040	0.0000	-0.0040	0.0058	-0.0030	0.0088
2025-30/2030-35	-0.0052	0.0000	-0.0052	0.0056	-0.0030	0.0086

Period	r(b)	r(f)	r(bf)	r(d)	r(l)	r(dl)
2030-35/2035-40	-0.0075	0.0000	-0.0075	0.0055	-0.0024	0.0079
2035-40/2040-45	-0.0066	0.0000	-0.0066	0.0053	-0.0024	0.0077
2040-45/2045-50	-0.0034	0.0000	-0.0034	0.0077	-0.0021	0.0098
LOW VARIANT PROJECTION						
1990-95/1995-2000	-0.0230	-0.0238	0.0007	-0.0213	-0.0078	-0.0135
1995-2000/2000-05	-0.0251	-0.0270	0.0018	-0.0213	-0.0069	-0.0144
2000-05/2005-10	-0.0277	-0.0320	0.0043	-0.0156	-0.0067	-0.0089
2005-10/2010-15	-0.0346	-0.0371	0.0025	-0.0083	-0.0050	-0.0033
2010-15/2015-20	-0.0434	-0.0456	0.0022	-0.0028	-0.0046	0.0018
2015-20/2020-25	-0.0015	0.0000	-0.0015	0.0084	-0.0037	0.0120
2020-25/2025-30	-0.0078	0.0000	-0.0078	0.0132	-0.0030	0.0163
2025-30/2030-35	-0.0114	0.0000	-0.0114	0.0124	-0.0030	0.0154
2030-35/2035-40	-0.0176	0.0000	-0.0176	0.0162	-0.0024	0.0186
2035-40/2040-45	-0.0192	0.0000	-0.0192	0.0170	-0.0024	0.0194
2040-45/2045-50	-0.0125	0.0000	-0.0125	0.0176	-0.0021	0.0197

A Comparison of Fertility Transition in China and India

Introduction

Around 1985, China and India, the two most populous countries of the World, accounted for more than 37 per cent of the World population (United Nations, 1991). Because of their sheer size of the population, future population prospects of the World will depend largely on the future population trends in the two countries. In the recent past, China has been able to achieve some signal successes in hastening the pace of demographic transition and in curtailing its population growth rate. On the other hand, in India, continued rapid population growth continues to be a major concern not only to the social and economic development of the country but also to the population growth of the World as a whole. Both China and India have interesting similarities and dissimilarities in terms of culture

175

and tradition, social and economic development and in the area of population control. In both countries, social and economic development is relatively low. Both countries have a very rich cultural and traditional heritage. Both countries have designed and implemented policies and programmes to modify population growth patterns so as to make them more conducive to social and economic progress. Both countries have made efforts to integrate population with development planning and in both countries, population control is an important component of the official development policy.

There are stark differences too between the two countries. India is the largest democracy in the World and is perhaps the only country in the developing World where democracy has been able to withstand all pressures and stresses. China, on the other hand is a communist country with an iron curtain. Government reigns a very strict control on the society as well as on every aspect of life in China. The two countries also differ in the level of demographic transition achieved. China has reached a very advanced stage of demographic transition. In India, there are little sings of such transition at present.

This paper is directed towards a comparison of the process of fertility transition in China and India since 1950. One of the objectives of this comparison is to identify salient positive and negative features of the course of fertility transition followed by the two countries and to identify the factors that appears to have been responsible for the particular paths. A second objective of the present analysis is to discuss the relevancy of the fertility transition paths of the two countries for other countries which are also trying to modify their population growth patterns.

176

Methodology

The key indicator used in this analysis is the growth rate in the number of births. This indicator has been selected in place of the conventional indicator, the growth rate of total population because it is very sensitive to fertility reduction efforts. The growth rate of total population, incidently, is not directly affected by these efforts. Since in both China and India, a major determinant of fertility transition has been official programmes to reduce fertility, an analysis based on the growth rate of number of births rather than growth of total population is expected to give a better insight into the fertility transition process.

Number of births in a particular year in any country is determined by the level of fertility and size and structure of the population. Following Horiuchi, total number of births in a particular year in a population can be represented as

$$B = N * TFR * (CBR/TFR) \qquad (1)$$

where B is the total number of births in a year, N is the total population in that year, TFR is the total fertility rate and CBR is the crude birth rate (Horiuchi, 1991). Denoting by r the growth rate of total live births, it is simple to show that

$$r_B = r_N + r_f + r_{bf} \qquad (2)$$

where f stands for total fertility rate and bf stands for the ratio CBR / TFR. Horiuchi has shown that the ratio CBR / TFR may be regarded as a measure of the age structure effect on the crude birth rate.

The above formulation suggests that the growth rate of total number of births in a population is the algebraic sum of the growth rate of total population, the growth rate of total fertility rate and the growth rate of the age structure effect on the crude birth rate. This means that the process of transition in the total number of births should be analysed in the context of the process of transition in total population size, level of fertility and in the process of transition in the age structure effect on the crude birth rate.

It is possible to improve the above formulation by observing that not the whole population is exposed to the risk of a birth. Since only females in the reproductive age are exposed to the risk of a birth, equations (1) and (2) can be modified as under:

$$B = W * TFR * (GFR/TFR) \qquad (3)$$

and

$$r_B = r_W + r_f + r_{gf} \qquad (4)$$

where W stands for total number of females in the reproductive age group and GFR is the general fertility rate. Here gf stands for the age structure effect on the general fertility rate.

The above formulation can also be used to analyse the components of relative change in the annual number of birth within the country over time. It can be shown that

$$B_2 / B_1 = N_2 / N_1 + TFR_2 / TFR_1 + ASE_2 / ASE_1 \qquad (5)$$
$$= W_2 / W_1 + TFR_2 / TFR_1 + ASE'_2 / ASE'_1 \qquad (6)$$

178

where subscripts stand for the beginning and the end of the period of reference and ASE is the age structure effect on crude birth rate while ASE' is the age structure effect on general fertility rate.

Data Source

Data for the present study have been taken from the United Nations data base developed by the Population Division of United Nations Department of International Economic and Social Affairs on the size and projection of population of the countries of the world. The 1990 revision of the data base includes information on population size, number of births every year, total fertility rate, crude birth rate proportion of females in the reproductive age group for each quinquennial period from 1950 through 2025 (United Nations, 1991). The reasons for opting for United Nations data base rather then for going for individual country sources of data are primarily that of the uniformity and comparability of the estimates prepared which is not the case when individual data sources are used for a comparative analysis as is the case here.

Results

Basic information on number of births per year, total fertility rate, crude birth rate etc. for the two countries is summarised in table 1. The two countries have observed entirely different trend in the total number of births since 1950. Average annual number of births in China decreased by about 13 per cent between 1950 and 1995. This decrease in the number of births per year has been associated with a 120 per cent increase in total population of the country, a 148 per cent increase in the number of women in the reproductive age group, a 68 per cent decrease in total fertility rate, a 56 per cent decrease in the crude birth rate and a 54 per cent decrease in the general fertility rate. By contrast, average annual number of births in India increased by about 57 per cent in between 1950 and 1995. This increase in average annual births per year has been associated with a 161 per cent increase in total population, a 165 per cent increase in females in the reproductive age group, a 37 per cent decrease in the total fertility rate, and a 34 per cent decrease in crude birth rate and 35 per cent decrease in the general fertility rate.

The trend in the average annual births has also not been the same in the two countries. In China, this trend is sharply fluctuating. In between 1950-55 and 1955-60, average annual births in China decreased sharply but increased rapidly during 1955-60 to 1965-70. In the next decade (1965-70 to 1975-80), average annual births again decreased very sharply. In between 1975-80 through 1985-90, average annual number of births in the again increased, first slowly and then sharply but after 1985-90, the number decreased again. In India, on the other hand, average annual number of births increased throughout the period 1950-1995 but amount of increase varied widely. During the period 1950-55 through 1970-75, average annual number of births in the country increased monotonically, at a very slowly decreasing rate of increase. During the short period between 1970-75 and 1975-80, there had been a very small increase in the average annual number of births but during the period 1975-80 to 1980-85, average annual number of births increased very sharply. In period, increase in the average annual number of births in the country was highest.

In table 2, relative change in annual number of births between 1950-55 and 1990-95 and its components has been presented for the two countries. A very drastic reduction in the total fertility rate in China has been found to be chiefly responsible for the reduction in the annual number of births between 1950 and 1995. Over a period of 45 years, the total fertility rate in the country decreased by more than two third - from 6.11 in 1950-55 to just 1.95 in 1990-95. Similarly, the general fertility rate in the country decreased by about 64 per cent - from 186 in 1950-55 to 68 in 1990-95. This drastic reduction in fertility levels in the country could be possible due to a very strong fertility control programme, especially during the period 1965-70 through 1975-80. Interestingly, the trend in total fertility rate has not been uniform. Like the total number of births, total fertility rate also increased and decreased during different sub-periods in between 1950 and 1995. In fact, most of the fertility reduction in China is confined to the period 1970-75 to 1975-80 when the total fertility rate in the country decreased by 2.68 absolute points. In India, however, fertility reduction of such a magnitude could not be achieved. Total fertility rate, in the country, decreased by just 37 per cent during the 45 years under reference while the general fertility rate decreased by about 35 per cent. In fact, reduction in fertility levels in the country was not large enough to compensate for net addition of births every year due to increase in population or due to increase in the number of women in the reproductive age group. As the result, average annual number of births increased throughout the period 1990-95. But the trend in total fertility rate and in general fertility rate is more smooth than the trend observed in China. In general, the absolute amount of decrease in total fertility rate increased in every five-year period in India with the only exception of the period 1975-80 to 1980-85 and 1985-90 to 1990-95.

The fluctuating trend in total fertility rate and general fertility rate in China is well reflected in the crude birth rate. Most of the decrease in crude birth rate in China has virtually been confined to two periods only - 1950-55/1955-60 and 1970-75/1975-80. In the remaining periods, decline in birth rate has been either very slow or there had been an increase in the crude birth rate. In India, by contrast, the decrease in crude birth rate has been more uniform. Up to 1975-80, not only crude birth rate declined monotonically but the absolute amount of decline in every sub-period also increased with time. This continuity in the pattern of decline in crude birth rate was broken during the period 1980-85. During the period 1980-85/1985-90, the amount of decrease in the crude birth rate increased again but this amount of decrease was lower than what was achieved during 1970-75/1975-80.

In both the countries, age structure effects on crude birth rate or on generally fertility rate have been positive throughout the period 1950-95. This indicates that the age structure of the population in both the countries has contributed in increasing the growth rate in the number of births. In both the countries, the age structure effects on either crude birth rate or on general fertility rate showed a decreasing trend up to the period 1970-75 but after 1975, the age structure effects on various indicators of fertility have tended to increase. In China, this increase has been very sharp. Because of this very sharp increase in the age structure effects on crude birth rate, the crude birth rate increased from 20.6 births per 1000 population in 1980-85 to 22.2 births per 1000 population during the period 1985-90 despite the fact that total fertility rate decreased from 2.50 to 2.41 during the same period. In India, by contrast, the age structure effects on crude birth rate or on general fertility rate have remained more or less unchanged. In the 45 years between 1950 and 1995, the age structure effects ion crude birth rate in India increased from 7.387 in 1950 to 7.760 in 1995 - an increase of just 0.475 absolute points.

The contribution of the size of population to the relative change in the annual number of births in both the countries has been found to be substantial in both the countries. Moreover, the change in the size of the population, expectedly, has acted towards increasing the annual number of births. In Chine, this effect of population momentum has been balanced by the steep reduction in total fertility rate but in India, reduction in the total fertility rate was not sufficient enough to balance the increase in the number of births due to the increase in the size of the population. Clearly, main factor behind the reduction in annual number of births in China has been a drastic reduction in the fertility of Chinese women as measured by the total fertility rate.

In table 3, the fertility transition path of the two countries has been described by calculating the growth rate of number of births as well as its various components for each quinquennial period beginning from 1950-55 separately for the two countries. Because the number of births is estimated for quinquennial period, the growth rate is computed as an average annual rate of increase from one quinquennial period to the next. In China, the trend does not appear to be very simple; it has both a downturn and an upturn. After a negative growth of the number of births during 1950-55/1955-60, there has been a very substantial increase in growth rate during 1955-60/1965-70 and then decreased very rapidly during the period 1965-70 to 1975-80. During the period 1975-80 to 1985-90, the trend in the number of births reversed again and, instead of decreasing, number of births actually increased. After 1985-90, there has been a noticeable decrease in total number of births, again.

In India, on the other hand, growth rate of the number of births showed a continuously declining trend since 1950-55 up to 1975-80. But during the period 1975-80/1980-85, there has been very sharp increase in this growth rate. Incidently, growth rate of the number of live births during the period 1975-80/1980-85 has been highest in the country since 1955. However, the rate of decline in the growth rate has been very slow and the rate has always been positive suggesting a continuous increase in the number of births per year. Main reason for this slow transition in the annual number of births in India has been a very slow decline in fertility. Between 1975 and 1984, total fertility rate in India declined by only 0.4 absolute points - from 4.9 children per woman to 4.5 children per woman in 1984 (Government of India, 1988).

In brief, the steep decline in the growth rate of number of births in China during the 1970s seems to be mainly attributable to a very sharp decline in fertility in China whereas in India, continued increase in the number of births every year appears to be a direct implication of a very slow decline in fertility of Indian women.

A question remains as to why the growth rate of the number of births in both the countries increased around 1980s (1975-

80/1980-85) as compared to the growth rate around mid-1970s (1970-75/1975-80). A decomposition of the growth rate of the number of births in table 3 suggests different reasons for the two countries.

In China, slow down of fertility decline appears to be the main reason for an increase in the growth rate of the number of births. There has practically been no change in total fertility rate in China between 1980-85 and 1985-90, a decrease of just 0.09 absolute points. At the same time, there has been a very substantial influx of females in the reproductive age group during this period as the result of very high fertility in the past. As discussed earlier, the CBR/TFR ratio is a measure of age structure effects on crude birth rate, and in turn, the number of births. In China, the growth rate of CBR/TFR has been rising during the past few decades implying that the age structure of Population in China has been increasingly in favour of a larger number of births relative to the population size and level of total fertility rate. This observation is also confirmed by the trend in the growth rate of GFR/TFR ratio.

In India too, both these reasons appear to be responsible for the upturn in growth rate of the number of births around 1980s. Fertility remained more or less stagnant during the period. The sample registration data, although associated with some error of under registration, showed that the general fertility rate in the country declined from 150.4 births per 1000 females in the reproductive age group in 1975 to only 145.2 births per 1000 females in the reproductive age group in 1984 (Government of India, 1988). There are indications that fertility in India continues to decline but this decline in fertility has been extremely slow. Similarly, like China, in India too, the age

185

structure effects on crude birth rate as well as on general fertility rate have increasingly been in favour of larger number of larger number of births relative to the population size and level of total fertility rate.

The age structure effects seems attributable mainly to the accelerated growth of female population in the reproductive age group. This accelerated growth may be due to the influx into the reproductive period of the cohorts born in the 1950s and 1960s - the period of so-called "population explosion". In addition, decreasing proportion of young population, caused by fertility decline, has also raised the proportion of other age groups, including the reproductive period.

But the age structure effects do not explain the short - term rise of growth rate of number of births in both the countries - in between mid 1970s and around 1980. At best they can be considered as a medium term trend contributing significantly to the relatively high level of growth rate of number of births around 1980.

Conclusions

Despite having very similar demographic situation around 1950, China and India have reached different stages of demographic transition. Still, the transition path of the two countries have many similarities. In both the countries, age structure effects on crude birth rate and general fertility rate have increasingly been in favour of the increase in the number of births given the size of the population and the level of fertility as measured by the total fertility rate. In both the countries, there has been an uptrend in the growth rate of number of births during the 1980s though the causes for this uptrend may be different.

Perhaps, the most important feature of the transition path of the two countries is its sensitiveness to official programme and policy and hence to the political commitment to the cause of fertility reduction. A description of the evolution of the evolution of policies and programmes for fertility reduction and its impact on the transition path of fertility in the two countries is not the scope of this paper but some of the important features of this evolution may be discussed.

An important factor that comes out of the present analysis is the impact of 1974 world population conference on population policy and programmes of the two countries. It appears that the consensus arrived at the 1974 conference had forced the political leadership of both the countries to put extra efforts to the cause of fertility reduction. That these efforts paid rich dividend is clear from table 3 as there was very substantial plunge in the growth rate of number of births as well as total fertility rate in both the countries. In India, for example, the government adopted a new but much more stringent population policy in 1976. As a result of the government emphasis, 11 million people were sterilized in just 22 months between 1975 and 1977 (Soni, 1984). In China, similarly, Mao, in the year 1974 indicated his support for the population policy saying 'population growth has to be controlled'. In the same year, the State Council's Leading Group on Family Planning issued a circular stating that contraceptives should be issued free of charge. In 1978, the plenary session of the Eleventh Central Committee declared family planning should be considered to be strategically important for the realization of the four modernizations - agriculture, industry, defence, and science and technology. The result of all these efforts was that the crude birth rate which was 31 per thousand in 1971 fell down to 18 per thousand in 1979 (United Nations, 1989).

But the story after 1977-78 is different for China and India. China continued her efforts to reduce fertility levels further through the introduction of one child policy in 1980. But in India, family planning became a politically sensitive issue during the general elections of 1977 in which the ruling party was defeated; its losses were heaviest in the central - north India where the programme had been most aggressively pursued. Most of the actions of the new government were directed towards the task of eradicating worst excesses of the Emergency, with a notable lack of positive measure to boost up the programme. Though, fertility control remained a priority issue on the development agenda of the country yet lack of political will, combined with the demoralisation of public servants implementing the programme, brought it to a virtual standstill resulting in a steep increase in the growth rate of number of births.

One can therefore foresee the importance of political commitment to the cause of fertility reduction as one of the essential preconditions for demographic transition. But in a democratic set-up, political commitment to fertility reduction has the risk of becoming a politically sensitive issue as it became in India. In such countries, the fear of political backlash during the elections considerably restricts the political support to fertility control activities. India is already suffering from this backlash as family planning in the country has reached a dead end with no body ready to take a bold initiative.

In China, fortunately, such fear does not exit mainly because of an entirely different system of government. In China, political support to fertility control has never been hesitant - either her political leaders denounced or they advocated family planning. This definiteness in political support to fertility control is well reflected in demographic transition in the country. When there was political support to the programme, the fertility control efforts performed exceedingly well. When political support was not there - during most of the Mao regime - these efforts performed very poorly. Clearly, in a democratic set up, demographic transition path is more risky than in a non-democratic set up. And there are only a few countries in the world today who advocate for a non-democratic set up.

References

China (1984) *Analysis of China's National One-per-thousand Fertility Survey.* Beijing, China Population Information Centre.

Government of India (1988) *A Handbook of Population Statistics.* New Delhi, Registrar General.

Horiuchi, S. (1991) Measurement and analysis of cohort-size variations. *Population Bulletin of the United Nations* 30: 160-24.

Jiang, Z. (1988) Reasons for fertility decline in China. Paper presented at the IUSSP Seminar on Fertility Transition in Asia: Diversity and Change. Bangkok, 28-31 March.

Soni, V. (1984) The development and current organisation of the family planning programme. In T. Dyson and N. Crook (eds) *India's Demography: Essays in Contemporary Population*. New Delhi, South Asian Publishers.

United Nations (1989) *China*. Population policy Paper No. 20, New York, Population Division.

United Nations (1991) *World Population Prospects 1990*. New York, United Nations.

Table 1:   Selected data on fertility in China and India

Year	Population (000)		CBR	TFR	GFR	Births (000)
	Total	Female (15-49)				
CHINA						
1950	554760	134252				
1955	609005	138244	43.6	6.11	185.93	25370
1960	657492	144648	35.9	5.48	160.63	22734
1965	729191	157505	37.8	5.61	173.39	26208
1970	830675	183579	36.9	5.94	168.88	28780
1975	927808	205973	28.3	4.76	127.77	24863
1980	998877	237733	21.5	3.26	93.48	20712
1985	1070175	278246	20.6	2.50	82.73	21292
1990	1155305	316554	22.2	2.41	83.15	24649
1995	1221462	333459	18.5	1.95	67.64	21988
INDIA						
1950	357561	84027				
1955	395096	93243	44.1	5.97	187.26	16589
1960	442344	103066	43.6	5.92	185.93	18235
1965	495157	113391	42.0	5.81	181.82	19669
1970	554911	126520	40.2	5.69	175.93	21122
1975	620701	142141	38.2	5.43	167.18	22448
1980	688856	159815	34.7	4.83	150.54	22727
1985	768185	179755	33.8	4.47	145.06	24617
1990	850638	201601	31.3	4.07	132.91	25339
1995	935744	222707	29.1	3.75	122.53	25988

Population and Development: The Indian Perspective

Table 2:   Ratio of births, population, etc. in China and India, 1950-55/1990-95

Variable	Ratio (1990-95/1950-55)	
	China	India
Births	0.867	1.567
Population	2.202	2.617
Females (15-49)	2.484	2.650
CBR	0.424	0.660
TFR	0.319	0.628
GFR	0.867	0.654
Age structure effects on CBR	1.330	1.051
Age structure effects on GFR	1.140	1.042

Table 3: Growth rate of total number of births and its decomposition in China and India, 1950-95.

Period	r_B	r_N	r_W	r_f	r_{bf}	r_g	r_{gf}
CHINA							
1950-55/1955-60	-2.19	1.69	0.75	-2.18	-1.71	-2.93	-0.75
1955-60/1960-65	2.84	1.81	1.32	0.47	0.56	1.53	1.06
1960-65/1965-70	1.87	2.35	2.42	1.14	-1.63	-0.53	-1.67
1965-70/1970-75	-2.93	2.40	2.66	-4.43	-0.88	-5.58	-1.15
1970-75/1975-80	-3.65	1.83	2.60	-7.57	2.07	-6.25	1.32
1975-80/1980-85	0.55	1.43	3.02	-5.31	4.45	-2.44	2.87
1980-85/1985-90	2.93	1.46	2.84	-0.73	2.23	0.10	0.83
1985-90/1990-95	-2.28	1.32	1.78	-4.24	0.59	-4.13	0.11
INDIA							
1950-55/1955-60	1.89	2.13	2.04	-0.17	-0.06	-0.14	0.03
1955-60/1960-65	1.51	2.26	1.95	-0.38	-0.37	-0.45	-0.07
1960-65/1965-70	1.43	2.27	2.06	-0.42	-0.46	-0.66	-0.24
1965-70/1970-75	1.22	2.26	2.26	-0.94	-0.09	-1.02	-0.09
1970-75/1975-80	0.25	2.16	2.34	-2.34	0.42	-2.10	0.25
1975-80/1980-85	1.60	2.13	2.35	-1.55	1.02	-0.74	0.81
1980-85/1985-90	0.58	2.11	2.32	-1.87	0.34	-1.75	0.12
1985-90/1990-95	0.51	1.97	2.13	-1.64	0.18	-1.63	0.01

A Parametric Investigation of Female Reproductive Age Mortality in India

Introduction

The introduction of reproductive health issues in the strategies and programmes addressed towards demographic transition has raised the need of measuring and analysing trends in the reproductive health status of the population, especially females. Reproductive morbidity and reproductive mortality are obviously the only indicators for monitoring the progress of 'Reproductive Health' initiative. Reproductive mortality is defined as the risk of death due to causes related to pregnancy and child birth and is commonly known as maternal mortality. Measurement of reproductive mortality, however, is most problematic in those countries where it has been estimated to be highest. A death due to causes associated with pregnancy and child birth is relatively a rare event. At the same time it is very difficult to classify whether a death is due to the factors associated with pregnancy and child birth or due to other factors. As such, even if the death registration is satisfactory, measurement of this risk remains difficult because of the problems of classification. At the same time, in most of the countries having exceptionally high levels of reproductive mortality, the death registration remains poor and so the estimates based on the registered deaths are gross underestimates of the actual situation. The alternative to registration, the population-based sample survey is also not feasible for estimating reproduction associated mortality. Since deaths due to factors associated with pregnancy and child birth are rare, an extremely large sample size as well as an accurate reporting by the respondents is required for estimating reproduction associated mortality. Retrospective surveys are not of much help because of the problems associated with the classification of deaths.

Because of the problems associated with the measurement of reproductive mortality through conventional approaches, a number of alternatives have been suggested which provide rapid estimates of the risk of death due to factors associated with pregnancy and child birth. In this paper, we review these approaches and propose a new approach with its application to India.

Measurement of Reproductive Mortality

According to World Health Organization, death associated with reproduction is defined as death of a woman while pregnant or within 42 days of the termination of pregnancy, irrespective of the duration of pregnancy, from any cause related to or aggravated by the pregnancy or its management but not from accidental or incidental causes (WHO, 1979).

Reproductive mortality, the risk of death associated with reproduction, can be measured in two ways. The reproductive mortality ratio relates the number of maternity associated deaths to the number of live births. The reproductive mortality rate, on the other hand, relates the number of maternity associated deaths to number of women in the reproductive age group. The rate indicates the risk of dying for females from maternity related causes while the ratio measures the obstetric risk in the population. Both the rate as well as the ratio are important. The rate measures the relative importance of reproductive deaths to total female deaths while the ratio is suitable for comparing mortality risks related to pregnancy between female populations at different levels of fertility.

The two indicators of the risk of death during pregnancy and child birth are closely related. Suppose, during a given period of time, in a population of women $P_f(x)$ aged x, $B(x)$ live births and $D_m(x)$ reproduction associated deaths are observed. Then the reproductive mortality rate at age x, t(x) is

$$t(x) = D_m(x) / P_f(x) \qquad (1)$$

while the ratio at age x, r(x) is

$$r(x) = D_m(x) / B(x) \qquad (2)$$

It is clear from equations (1) and (2) that

$$t(x) = r(x) * f(x) \qquad (3)$$

where f(x) is the female birth rate at age x.

For the whole reproductive period, equation (3) reduces to

$$T = R*GFR \qquad (4)$$

Where T is the rate, R is the ratio and GFR is the general fertility rate. Thus knowing either rate or ratio, the other indices can be calculated.

Both rate and ratio are affected by the age pattern of fertility. Births at youngest and oldest ages of the reproductive life span, as well as at high parity, imply high mortality risk for women. However, the effects of age and parity distribution of fertility on the reproductive mortality ratio are not very large.

Methods of Measurement of Reproductive Mortality

Methods suggested to overcoming the problems associated with the estimation of reproduction associated mortality through conventional data can be divided into two groups. First group of methods consists in enlarging the size of the sample by collecting information on more than one reproductive deaths from one respondent. The other approach consists of the analysis of the age specific death rates. This analysis is carried out in two ways - 1) comparing the age pattern of mortality of males and females and 2) analysing the female age pattern of mortality alone.

The sisterhood method and networking are the two approached that have been suggested to enlarge the sample. The sisterhood method consists in asking questions from the respondents about their sister's mortality experience so that each interviewed person becomes a respondent for several females (Graham et. al. 1989). The method is an extension of siblings survival technique (Hill and Trussel, 1977). Trussel and Rodriguez (1990) has further suggested that questions may also be asked from adult brothers about their sister's mortality experience.

Another technique suggested by Boerma and Mati (1989) is based on the identification of reproduction associated deaths through "networking ". This method is based on the assumption that reproduction associated deaths are important social events in the community and many women in the community are likely to have heard about them and remember some details. As such, a network of households with possible reproduction associated deaths can be constructed. This network can then be visited to interview the relatives of the deceased woman.

Both the sisterhood method as well as the networking approach require primary data for the estimation of reproduction associated mortality. This means that if the monitoring system is to be based on these methods, repeated surveys at specific intervals are to be carried out to estimate the level as well as the trend in the risk of death due to causes related to pregnancy and child birth.

The second approach of estimating reproductive mortality is based on the analysis of age pattern of mortality. This analysis can be carried out in two ways. First methods is based on the analysis of mortality sex ratios during the reproductive life span (Blum and Fargues, 1990). This method, however, is dependent upon the male mortality level and so is not termed as an appropriate approach to measure reproductive mortality.

Alternatively, the risk of death due to complications of pregnancy and child birth can be measured through the analysis of female mortality curve itself. It is well known that female age pattern of mortality shows a hump during the reproductive life span. This hump may be attributed to reproduction associated mortality. Analysis of the size and shape of this hump, therefore, can give useful information about the risk of death due to factors associated with pregnancy and child birth. Blum and Fargues (1990) have proposed two approaches to analyse this hump and to estimate reproduction associated mortality. Their approaches are based on an extrapolation by smoothing the observed profile of woman's mortality. Implicit in both the approaches is the assumption that woman's mortality at child bearing ages consists mainly of reproductive deaths. If mortality from accidents and injuries is important, a bias will be introduced which will affect estimates.

Methods based on female age-specific death rates provide a quick idea of the level and trends of female reproductive age mortality from which the risk of death of death due to factors associated with pregnancy and child birth can be estimated if some information about the proportion of reproductive deaths to the total deaths in the reproductive age group is known. Thus, an analysis of the age pattern of mortality provides a relatively simple way of assessing reproductive mortality. Since information on age-specific death rates by sex is now increasingly available in almost all the countries with poor vital registration, these methods can be made a basis for developing a monitoring system for 'Reproductive Health Initiative'.

A Parametric Investigation of Reproductive Age Mortality
Heligman and Pollard (1980) has suggested that age curve of mortality essentially consist of three separate curves. The first curve deals with infant and child mortality and its contribution rapidly declines with advancing age. The second curve describes the middle life mortality, especially the hump in middle ages and shows steep declines as the curve is extended on both side of the hump. The third and final component of the age curve of the mortality is the Gompertz function that takes care of the mortality at older ages.

Of particular interest here is the second component of Heligman and Pollard mortality schedule. This component estimates the middle life mortality. It reflects the accident mortality in males and accident plus reproduction associated mortality in females, i.e. additional mortality superimposed on the 'natural curve of mortality' as described by the other two components. Heligman and Pollard has used the following function to approximate the youth and adult life mortality hump

$$_1q_x = D^{-E(\ln(x) - \ln(F))^2} \qquad (5)$$

where x represents the age, $_1q_x$ is the probability of death between age x to x+1, and D, E and F are the parameters of the equation to be estimated. Parameter F indicates the location of the middle age mortality; E represents its spread and D the severity. This is a log-normal function with maximum value of D at age x=F, declining on either side of this age. The function is symmetric function of ln(x) but not of x. It declines more slowly for ages above x=F.

The parameters D, E and F provide valuable insight into the female reproductive age mortality. In addition, if the information about the proportion of reproductive deaths to all female deaths during the reproductive life span are known, further adjustments in the level of reproductive age mortality rate can be made to obtain the reproduction associated mortality rate. Finally, reproductive mortality ratio can be obtained from the reproductive mortality rate through the knowledge of age-specific birth rate or general fertility rate.

The only requirement in the application of the above approach for the analysis of the reproductive age mortality is the estimation of the parameters of equation (5). One way of estimating these parameters is to fit the Heligman-Pollard model mortality schedule to observed age-specific probabilities of death. Normally fitting of Heligman-Pollard model mortality schedule requires single year probabilities of death. If the probability of death is available for conventional five year age groups then the Heligman-Pollard model mortality schedule can be fitted through the application of the UNABR routine of MORTPAK computer software package developed by the United Nations (United Nations, 1988). Application of the routine gives the estimates of all the seven parameters of Heligman-Pollard model mortality schedule which include the parameters D, E and F also. Once parameters of the equation (5) are estimated, estimation of reproductive age mortality rate as well as reproduction associate mortality rate and ratio is a simple exercise. In India, probabilities of death are available for conventional five year age groups through the Sample

Registration System and not for the single year age groups so the UNABR routine has been applied for the characterisation of the reproductive age mortality.

Reproductive Age Mortality in India

We have applied the above approach to analyse and characterize the reproductive age mortality in India during the period 1983-93. Data used for the analysis are the age specific death rates obtained through the Sample Registration System for the year 1983 through 1993. The age specific death rates available from the Sample Registration system were smoothed through a three years moving average process to eliminate year to year random fluctuations. Estimates of parameters of middle life mortality - parameters D, E and F for different years of the period 1983-93 are shown in table 1. An important feature of the table is a totally contrasting trend in parameters D and E prior to 1990 and after 1990. In case of the parameter D which reflects the highest mortality during the middle life, a sharp declining trend prior to 1990 can easily be noticed from table 1 but after 1990, this downward trend is totally reversed and instead of decreasing the value of the parameter D has increased.

In case of parameter E, the trend is opposite to that of the parameter D. This is expected as this parameter measures the concentration of middle life mortality at its peak value - the higher is the value of the parameter, the higher is the concentration and vice versa. As may be seen from table 1, this parameter has shown a nearly monotonically increasing trend up to 1990 suggesting that the mortality during the adulthood has tended to be concentrated more and more around its peak value. However, after 1990, this parameter, instead of increasing has started decreasing. This indicates an increase in the dispersion of adulthood mortality and the adult mortality curve becoming platokurtic in nature.

Finally, the parameter F which shows the age at which the highest adult mortality occurs has shown a fluctuating trend. From 1983-85 to 1986-88, the value of the parameter F has decreased, first slowly and then rapidly. This indicates that the peak of the adult age mortality has shifted towards the left - to younger ages. This shift reflects the influence of the family planning activities as the result of which the proportion of lower parity birth has increased (the birth limitation impact). However, after achieving the lowest value during 1986-88, the value of the parameter increased sharply during 1987-89 and then decreased sharply again during 1988-90. After 1988-90, the value of the parameter increased again which indicates that the influence of family planning appears to have waned.

In table 2, we have presented estimates of female reproductive age mortality rate and female reproductive age mortality ratio for different periods of the reference period. These estimates have been derived on the basis of the parameters D, E and F estimated on the basis of age specific death rates available through the sample registration system. During the period 1983-85, the female reproductive age mortality rate in the country has been estimated to be approximately 261 female deaths for every 100000 female in the reproductive age group. This rate declined almost monotonically to 169 female deaths for every 100000 females in the reproductive age group by the period 1988-90. However, beyond the period 1988-90, the rate has started increasing and by the period 1991-93, the rate had increased to 188 female deaths for every 100000 females in the reproductive age group.

Once female reproductive age mortality rate is estimated, the reproduction associated mortality rate as well as reproduction associated mortality ratio or the risk of death due to factors associated with pregnancy and child birth can be estimated if the proportion of reproduction deaths to total female deaths in the reproductive age group is known.

An important issue in estimating reproduction associated mortality ratio through the analysis of female age-pattern of mortality, therefore, is to estimate the proportion of deaths due to the complications of pregnancy and child birth out of the total female deaths in the reproductive age group. As already discussed, this issue is quite complicated because of the problems of classification of a death of a female during the reproductive age as a reproduction associated death in India. In societies where interval between successive births is very short and where level of social and economic development is poor, as is the case with India, it can be argued that majority of the female deaths during the reproductive period are reproduction associated deaths. On the other hand, in situations where fertility is low and where an advanced stage of social and economic development has been achieved, reproduction associated female deaths may be assumed to contribute only marginally to overall female mortality in the reproductive age group. In this context, estimates obtained through the analysis of age-pattern of mortality may be thought of as the upper limit of reproductive mortality.

Information about the proportion of reproduction associated deaths to total female deaths in the reproductive age group is generally not available. For India, information about the proportion of reproductive deaths to all female deaths in the child bearing period is available on the basis of a study carried out in one district of South India (Bhatia, 1993). If it is assumed that the pattern observed in one district is applicable to the whole country, estimates of reproduction associated mortality rate can be obtained from reproductive mortality rate. These rates are given in the second column of table 2. These refined estimates of reproductive mortality ratio are presented in the last column of table 2 which suggest that the reproduction associated mortality rate in the country reduced from 93 reproduction associated deaths for every 100000 females in the reproductive age group to 72 reproduction associated deaths for every 100000 females in the reproductive age group in between the period 1983-85 and 1991-93. This means that over a period of ten years, the reproduction associated mortality rate has decreased by 21 absolute points. This implies that, on average, approximately 2 reproduction associated deaths for every 100000 females in the reproductive age group could be prevented.

Once reproduction associated mortality rate is estimated, the reproduction associated mortality ratio can be obtained by dividing the reproduction associated mortality rate by the general fertility rate. The estimates of reproduction associated mortality ratio so obtained are given in the last column of table 2. Our estimates suggest that the reproduction associated mortality ratio in the country was about 651 reproduction associated deaths for every 100000 live births during the period 1983-85. This ratio is estimated to have reduced to 608 reproduction associated deaths for every 100000 live births by the period 1991-93. In other words, over a period of 10 years, the reproduction associated deaths in the country reduced by 43 absolute points for every 100000 live births. This means that, during the ten years between 1983 and 1993, for every 100000 live births, only 43 reproduction associated deaths could be prevented in the country as a whole. It appears that there has practically been little change in the risk of death due to factors associated with pregnancy and child birth during the period 1983-93.

Conclusions

The main purpose of the paper was to suggest a simple approach which can be the basis for the monitoring of the reproductive health programmes that have now been adopted universally. The method suggested here may be viewed as a rapid estimation approach. it has the advantage over the other such methods in the sense that it requires little technical expertise and no primary data. Since, the software package required for the estimation purpose is already available, its application is a simple exercise.

Application of the approach to the Indian data suggests that there has been practically little reduction in the risk of death due to factors associated with pregnancy and child birth in eighties and early nineties and this risk appears to increasing after 1990. The analysis carried out here also indicates that whatever little reduction in the reproduction associated mortality is there, most of it has been confined to the later ages of the reproductive period. In the younger ages of the reproductive period, there appears to be very little change in the risk of reproduction associated deaths. Although, an exploration of the reasons behind the increase in the risk of deaths due to factors associated with reproduction is not the scope of this paper yet, it appears that the stress on births limitation in the National Family Welfare Programme has influenced the risk of reproduction associated to some extent. In any case, there is a need to analyse determinants of reproduction associated morbidity and mortality for a more effective implementation of the reproductive health initiative.

References

Bhatia JC (1993) Levels and causes of maternal mortality in Southern India. *Studies in Family Planning* 24(5): 310-18.

Blum A, Fargues P(1990) Rapid estimations of maternal mortality in countries with defective data. An application to Bomako (1974-85) and other developing countries. *Population Studies* 44: 155-71.

Boerma JT, Mati JKG (1989) Identifying maternal mortality through networking: Results from Coastal Kenya. *Studies in Family Planning* 20(5): 245-53.

Graham W, Brass W, Snow RW (1980) Estimating maternal mortality: The sisterhood method. *Studies in Family Planning* 20(3): 125-35.

Heligman L, Pollard JH (1980) The age pattern of mortality. *Journal of Institute of Actuaries* 107: 49-80.

Hill K, Trussell J (1977) Further developments in indirect mortality estimation. *Population Studies* 31: 313-24.

Trussell J, Rodriguez G (1990) A note on the sisterhood estimator of maternal mortality. *Studies in Family Planning* 21(6): 344-45.

United Nations (1988) *MORTPAK - The United Nations Software Package for Mortality Measurement*. New York, United Nations.

Table 1: Parameters of Heligman-Pollard Mortality schedule for India females: 1983-93.

Period	D	E	F
1983-85	0.00321	1.34	24.04
1984-86	0.00317	1.42	23.85
1985-87	0.00298	1.82	23.31
1986-88	0.00275	2.21	21.98
1987-89	0.00284	2.19	23.09
1988-90	0.00265	2.56	21.91
1989-91	0.00269	2.61	22.81
1990-92	0.00272	2.50	23.29
1991-93	0.00271	2.41	23.45

Table 2: Reproduction Associated Mortality Rate and Ratio for India: 1973-93

Period	Female Reproductive Age Mortality Rate	Reproduction associated mortality	
		Rate	Ratio
1983-85	261	93	651
1984-86	254	91	649
1985-87	223	82	605
1986-88	185	72	539
1987-89	200	76	584
1988-90	169	67	530
1989-91	178	70	564
1990-92	185	71	593
1991-93	188	72	608

Population and Development: The Indian Perspective

Status of Women in India
Variation Across States

Introduction

The world has always been a place of diversities, inequalities and dualities. The yawning gap between the North and the South of the World is the starkest dualism of our times so much so that each can easily be regarded as a separate planet. Yet, all these diversities, inequalities and dualities have one thing in common - a built-in bias for males that translates into varying degrees of prejudice against females. These prejudices are blatant in some areas, subtle in others without any consideration to prosperity or penury. The fact is that females, who constitute one half of World's population and one third of official labour force, perform nearly two thirds of work hours and, according to some estimates, receive only one third of World's income and own less than one hundredth of World property. Throughout the World women face an insidious and

213

drastic disparity with their own menfolk. The secondary status accorded to women becomes, under the conditions of poverty and hunger, a battle for survival in most of the developing countries.

India, the second largest democracy in the World, is a *World* in itself. Diversities over culture, society, religion, incomes etc. are perhaps sharpest in India than in any other country of the World. Since times immemorial, India has attracted people of different cultures and societies as merchants, as missionaries and as intruders. As the result, the Indian society, today, is a very complex mix of different religions and cultures and different ways of life. This religious and cultural complexity of the country along with differentials in levels of social and economic development, almost automatically, imply distinct differences in the position of women in the community, family and society. One may also expect these differences to be quite strong and persistent over time because of the persistence of the diversity in social and cultural settings and social and economic development. Any discussion on the status of women in India, therefore, requires a regional perspective.

Using the available information, this paper is directed toward a comparative analysis of the status of women in different States of the country. Another objective of the present paper is to explore the factors that are expected to contribute to different cultural, social, religious and economic values accorded to the fair sex at the family, community and society level in different parts of the country. In this context, the paper compares at length the situation prevailing in Tamilnadu, a State having a relatively better status of women and Gujrat, a state with relatively poor status of women.

214

Measurement of the Status of Women

There is no clearly defined as well as measurable definition of the status of women; it is a very generalised term which may be interpreted in different ways in different contexts. A number of demographic, kinship and family, economic and social variables have been used to characterize the position of women in the family, community and society. Because of this complexity, no single indicator can capture the variation in the status of women widely prevalent in every society. In an attempt to prepare a comprehensive list of indicators which encompass all aspects of status of women, Mason has suggested a list of 34 indicators (Mason, 1984). It has also been observed that the variability in the status of women across the World can be characterised along three dimensions - the dimension of health and education, the dimension of social equality and dimension of economic Independence (Chaurasia, 1994). The problem, however, is that in most of the developing countries information related to social equality and economic independence of females is rarely available. In such a situation, the alternative is to use the proxy variables.

We have used a set of 13 variables to measure the status of women and have analysed the variation in the status woman across the States of the country as measured by these variables. These variables are grouped into three dimensions - dimension of health and education, dimension of social equity and dimension of economic independence. The list of variables used in the analysis are given in table 1. The only criterion for the selection of the variables was their availability. As stressed earlier, availability of suitable information is a major constraint in any analysis of the status of women.

215

The analysis presented in this paper has followed the following lines:

- In order to assess the position of woman in the society, information was collected on the thirteen variables described above for fourteen major States of the country.

- In order to resolve the problem of aggregation, a simple ranking approach was used. For each of the thirteen variables, the States were ranked from best to poorest. The State having the best level for a given indicator was given rank one and vice versa.

- Having ranked all the States on all the indicators of the status of woman in such a way, the average rank of each State was obtained by adding ranks obtained in different variables of and dividing the sum by the number of indicators. All the variables included in this analysis were given equal weights in this exercise. Moreover, this exercise was carried out for all variables simultaneously as well as for the three dimensions separately.

- The average rank so obtained has been termed as the relative index of the status of women. It is clear from the nature of the construction that the index takes values between 1 and 14. If a State has its index equal to 1 than this means that the State has best level of all indicators among the 14 States under considered here. On the other hand, if the index is equal to 14, then this means that the State concerned has poorest level in all the indicators. If, the level of an indicator is reflective of the status of women then this index gives a comparative idea of position of women in the cultural, social, and economic milieu of the different States.

Findings

The relative index of the status of women for different States of the country is given in table 2 separately for the three dimensions of the status of women and for all the three dimensions combined. It may be seen from the table that amongst the major States of the country, the status of women is comparatively best in Kerala as measured by the relative index of status of women. It has lowest relative index in all the three dimensions of the status of women. Other States where the relative index has been found to be less than 7 are Tamilnadu, Karnataka, Andhra Pradesh and Maharashtra Punjab and Gujrat. Four of these six States are in the south. In fact, in all the southern States of the country, the relative index has been found to be substantially less than 7 indicating that the status of women in these States is relatively better as compared to other States of the country.

In contrast to Kerala, the status of women has been found to be poorest in Bihar. Other States where the value of the relative index has been found to be more than 7 are Uttar Pradesh, Rajasthan, Haryana, Madhya Pradesh, Orissa and West Bengal. Interestingly, all these States are in the northern part of the country. Moreover, in the four Hindi speaking States - Uttar Pradesh, Bihar, Rajasthan and Madhya Pradesh, the value of the relative index has always been found to be more than 9.

It is clear from table 1 that there exists a north-south divide in the country as far as the status of women is concerned. All the States in the south are having relatively better status of women as compared to the States in the north as is reflected through the variation in the relative index. Dyson and Moore have also observed this north-south divide in the status of women in India in the 1970s and attributed this divide to kinship structure (Dyson and Moore, 1983). The important point to stress here is that despite all investments in the social and economic development targeted toward women during the last twenty years, this north-south divide has persisted over time in the country.

Table 2 also suggests that the States of the country vary widely on the three dimensions of the status of women. It is therefore interesting to explore the similarities and dissimilarities among the States on the three dimensions of the status of women. The cluster analysis technique was applied to explore the similarities and dissimilarities between States on the three dimensions of the status of women and the findings obtained are summarised in table 3 along with average relative indexes for each cluster on the three dimensions as well as on all dimensions combined.

It is also clear from the table that Kerala and Bihar both have typical pattern of status of women as characterized by the three dimensions and the two States are located at the two extremes of the status of women; Kerala is the best and Bihar is the worst. Table 3 also suggests that as one moves from the southern most State of the country towards the north, the status of women deteriorates and it becomes worst in the States of Uttar Pradesh and Bihar. The only exception to this pattern is the State of Punjab which is known for an advanced level of economic development.

Among the similarities presented in table 3, some interesting dissimilarities can also be observed. Most importantly, the status of women in the context of health and education appears to be slightly better in Bihar as compared to the States of Madhya Pradesh, Rajasthan and Uttar Pradesh. The reason appears to be related to more the problems with the data from Bihar than to any real difference. Similarly, the economic independence of women as measured by the work participation rate and proportion of female workers in the tertiary sector appears to be better in the States of cluster II as compared to the State of Kerala. The reason, probably, is an advanced level of economic development in the States of Punjab, Gujrat and Maharashtra, the three States included in the cluster.

Is there any relationship between the levels of social, economic and infrastructure development of a State and the status of women? In order to explore this relationship, we have also developed relative indexes of economic and social development for each State of the country by applying the same methodology which has been used for developing the relative indexes for the status of women. For developing the index of economic development, six variables have been used. On the other hand, five variables were used for developing the index of social development. The list of indicators of social and economic development used for developing the relative indexes is given in the appendix.

Population and Development: The Indian Perspective

Table 4 shows interesting similarities and dissimilarities in the level of development across the States of the country. In terms of economic development, Punjab is the most developed State while the economic development is least in Bihar. In case of social development, Kerala is the most developed State while Bihar is the poorest one. The table also suggests that, in general, economic development and social development are closely associated. This observation is also confirmed by a significant correlation coefficient between the index of economic development and index of social development. However, there are certain exceptions. In Kerala, for example, a relatively low level of economic development is associated with a very advanced level of social development. Similarly, in Haryana, a very advanced level of economic development is associated with a very low level of social development.

The Spearman's correlation coefficients between the indexes of the status of women and the indexes of development are given in table 5. Very interestingly, none of the indexes of the status of women is statistically significantly correlated with the index of economic development whereas all the indexes of status of women are statistically significantly correlated with the index of social development. This means that it is possible to achieve an advanced level of status of woman and a narrow gender difference even without achieving high levels of economic development. Kerala is the best example here. Kerala has been able to achieve an advanced level of social development without an advanced level of economic development. The advanced status of women in Kerala is the result of this advanced level of social development. The point to ponder is whether the experience of Kerala can be repeated in other States of the country. In other words, can improvements in the health and educational status be achieved without enhancing income levels. If it is possible then an improvement in woman's status can be achieved even without economic progress. The example of Kerala shows this is possible.

On the other hand, if the economic development does not lead to social development, then even the advanced level of economic development cannot ensure improved status of the women in the family and the society. The State of Haryana is perhaps the best example of this situation. Despite a very advanced level of economic development, this State has a poor level of social development and hence a low status of women. The same is true, to some extent, in the State of Gujrat also.

Thus, a relatively low status of woman and a relatively wide gender difference has been found to co-exit with relatively low levels of social development. However, the same cannot be said about economic development. There are a number of States in the country which have made considerable progress in economic front but they lag behind in social development. As a result the status of woman remains low and gender difference wide.

The case of Gujrat and Tamilnadu
What are the options, therefore, for improving status of women and reducing gender inequalities in India. This question can be discussed in the light of the experience in Gujrat and Tamilnadu. Tamilnadu is one of the southern most State of the country while Gujrat is located in the western corner. The two States have almost similar population size, similar level of urbanisation and very nearly same sex ratio of population. But

221

the status of women in Tamilnadu is far better than that in Gujrat. As such a comparison of the status of woman in the two States is expected to provide some information that may help in formulating recommendations for improving the status of woman.

In order to explore the above issues in some detail, we have summarised the indicators related to the status of women, gender equality, and social and economic development for Gujrat and Tamilnadu in tables 6 and 7 respectively to get a composite scenario that prevails in the two States. It may be seen from the table that out of 13 variables of status of woman, the situation is better in Gujrat in only one variable - under five mortality sex ratio - when compared to Tamilnadu. Clearly, by all aspects, the status of women as reflected by the 14 indicators given in table 6 is better in Tamilnadu as compared to Gujrat.

We thus find that a relatively advanced level of economic development in Gujrat has not resulted in a relatively advanced level of social or infrastructure development. Higher income levels in Gujrat are associated with more hospital beds and more doctors but less nurses, less roads per 100 square kilometre. These patterns are associated with poor health and educational status resulting in wider gender inequalities and lower status of women in Gujrat. By contrast, in Tamilnadu, despite low income levels, relatively advanced social and infrastructure development has been achieved. Clearly what Tamilnadu has achieved at low income levels, Gujrat has not been able to achieve even at comparatively high income levels.

It also appears that, despite relatively higher income levels, social and cultural orthodoxy associated with traditional customs and beliefs and societal norms are more strong in Gujrat than in Tamilnadu. As an example, the index of the practice of purdah in Gujart has been estimated to be 41.8 as compared to just 4.9 in Tamilnadu which clearly shows that women in Tamilnadu have relatively much more freedom than their counterpart in Gujrat. Similarly the index of son preference in Gujrat is 20.8 which is substantially higher than the index of son preference of 11.9 in Tamilnadu which shows that relative value of women in Gujrat is less than the value of their counterparts in Tamilnadu. These observations suggest that increase in income and associated infrastructure development in Gujrat does not appear to have resulted in that type of social transformation which is conducive to improving the status of women and society continues to be traditional as far as women's issues are concerned. However, this is not the case in Tamilnadu. In an earlier analysis of status of woman in developing countries, it has been concluded that increase in income and associated infrastructure development and facilities may not lead to social equality of women with men. Such a situation is amply reflected by the situation prevailing in Gujrat. (Chaurasia, 1994).

Policy implications
The foregoing analysis suggests that increase in income levels and associated infrastructure development may not ensure equality between men and women particularly when increased income is oriented more towards capital investment and concentration of services than when it is oriented towards human investment and diffusion of technology. Investment in capital may result in even further increase in income and

223

improved infra-structural facilities but not in improvement in the quality of life as has been the case in Gujrat.

What is therefore needed to improve the status of woman is an investment in the human beings and not capital investment. This investment in human beings should be such that it should be able to reach the unreached. It should not be concentrated in the form of big high technology hospitals, highly qualified doctors, facilities for higher education, etc. Rather, it should focus on equitable distribution of resources, probably in the form of appropriate low-cost technology which is affordable and accessible to even the poorest of the poor in the society. The case of Tamilnadu shows that necessary improvements in the quality of life can be ensured by investment in the human being even at low levels of economic development.

Finally, despite all talks of development, as this analysis shows, culture and tradition continue to dominate, in a substantial manner, the process of transition in the family, society and the community, that determine the status of woman, especially in those States of the country where the current levels of social and economic development are low. In these States, the need of the time is to focus on social development through investment in human beings rather than investments in capital formation and application of advanced, usually costly, technology.

References

Chaurasia AR (1994) Dimensions of status of woman in developing countries. *Journal of Family Welfare*, Vol 40 (3), pp 42-50.

Dyson T, Moore M (1983) On kinship structure, female autonomy and demographic behaviour in India. *Population and Development Review*, 9 (1), pp: 35-60.

Government of India (1994) *Health Information of India, 1994*. New Delhi, Central Health Intelligence Bureau.

Mason K (1984) *The status of women, fertility and mortality: A review of interrelationships*. New York, The Rockefeller Foundation.

Table 1:   Variables used in the measurement of the status of women.

Dimension I Health and Education	1. 2. 3. 4. 5. 6.	Female life expectancy at birth Female under 5 mortality rate Female literacy rate Total fertility rate Female mean age at marriage Sex ratio
Dimension II Social Equality	7. 8. 9. 10. 11.	Gender difference in life expectancy Gender difference in under 5 mortality Gender difference in literacy Gender difference in work participation rate Gender difference in proportion of workers in tertiary sector
Dimension III Economic Independence	12. 13.	Female work participation rate Proportion of female workers in tertiary sector

Table 2:   Relative Index of the Status of Women

| State | Dimensions | | | | Rank |
	I	II	III	Combined	
Andhra Pradesh	5.83	5.00	5.50	5.46	3
Bihar	11.17	11.20	12.00	11.31	14
Gujrat	6.50	7.00	7.00	6.77	7
Haryana	8.33	9.40	8.50	8.77	10
Karnataka	5.50	7.00	5.50	6.08	6
Kerala	1.00	3.60	5.50	2.69	1
Madhya Pradesh	11.83	8.80	7.50	10.00	11
Maharashtra	5.33	5.80	5.50	5.54	4
Orissa	8.50	7.20	8.00	7.92	9
Punjab	5.17	5.60	7.50	5.69	5
Rajasthan	11.67	9.80	9.50	10.62	12
Tamilnadu	3.33	6.60	4.50	4.77	2
Uttar Pradesh	12.50	9.60	11.00	11.15	13
West Bengal	8.33	6.40	7.50	7.46	8

Table 3:   Clustering of States on the Dimensions of Status of Women

Cluster	States in the cluster	Dimensions			
		I	II	III	All
I	Kerala	1.00	3.60	5.50	2.69
II	Karnataka, Maharashtra, Andhra Pradesh, Gujrat, Punjab, Tamilnadu	4.52	5.29	5.07	4.90
III	Haryana, Orissa, West Bengal	8.39	7.67	8.00	8.05
IV	Madhya Pradesh, Rajasthan, Uttar Pradesh	12.00	9.40	9.33	10.59
V	Bihar	11.17	11.20	12.00	11.31

Table 4:   Indexes of Economic and Social
                Development.

State	Economic Development		Social development	
	Index	Rank	Index	Rank
Andhra Pradesh	7.67	8	8.80	10
Bihar	13.00	13	12.20	13
Gujrat	6.83	5	6.20	7
Haryana	4.00	2	7.00	9
Karnataka	7.17	6	6.60	8
Kerala	8.33	10	1.20	1
Madhya Pradesh	8.00	9	12.00	11
Maharashtra	5.33	3	3.40	3
Orissa	11.00	12	11.20	11
Punjab	3.17	1	3.20	2
Rajasthan	7.33	7	11.20	11
Tamilnadu	6.17	4	4.60	4
Uttar Pradesh	8.67	11	11.80	12
West Bengal	8.33	10	5.60	6

Population and Development: The Indian Perspective

Table 5:   Correlation between indexes of status of
              women and indexes of development

Dimensions of status of women	Economic development index	Social development index
Dimensions I	0.197	0.597*
Dimension II	0.352	0.752**
Dimension III	0.424	0.570*
All dimensions	0.436	0.840**

*Significant at P=.05   ** Significant at P=.001

Table 6: Selected indicators of status of women in Gujrat and Tamilnadu

	Indicator	Gujrat	Tamilnadu
1.	Sex ratio	934	974
2.	Female mean age at marriage	19.0	19.1
3.	Female literacy rate	48.6	51.3
4.	Enrolment ratio (14-18) years	49.7	44.6
5.	Drop out rate (Primary)	56.7	38.2
6.	Total fertility rate	4.2	3.1
7.	Female child mortality rate	104	70
8.	Female expectation of life at birth	62.7	63.5
9.	Female work participation rate	26.0	29.9
10.	Child mortality sex ratio	107	109
11.	Expectation of life at birth sex ratio	103	100
12.	Labour force sex ratio	49	53
13.	Sex ratio of workers in tertiary sector	40	52
14.	Literacy sex ratio	66	70

Table 7:   Indicators of social and economic
             development in Gujrat and Tamilnadu

Indicator		Gujrat	Tamilnadu
A.	Social Development		
1.	Births attended by medically trained person	58.3	77.1
2.	Death rate	8.1	8.0
3.	Infant mortality rate	58	56
4.	Population served by government hospital	2008	1470
5.	Literacy (All ages)	61.3	62.7
3.	Economic Development		
1.	Per capita income (Rs)	2719	2349
2.	per cent of population below poverty line	18.4	32.8
3.	Per capita availability of food	131	151
4.	Per capita electricity consumption	450	342
5.	Roads per 100 Sq. Km	11.7	40.0
6.	Work participation rate	40.2	43.3

Appendix: Variables used for measuring the social and economic status.

Economic development	1.	Income per capita
	2.	Population below poverty line
	3.	Work participation rate
	4.	Per capita availability of food
	5.	Per capita electricity consumption
	6.	Roads per 100 sq km
Social development	7.	Crude death rate
	8.	Infant mortality rate
	9.	Population served by government hospital
	10.	Literacy rate
	11.	Deliveries attended by trained persons

Urbanisation in India
With Special Reference to Greater Bombay

Introduction

Urbanisation is an outcome of the process of transition in the economy and the society. The origin of the urbanisation process may be traced in the beginning of the trade - of agriculture or primary commodities - between population groups. Trade required outlet and inlet centres which were the first urban areas in the World. Later on urban centres developed in the context of religion, defence and administration also. With the advent of industrialisation, urbanisation process accelerated as industrialisation, among others, gave a big boost to the trade between as well as within countries.

Urban population has many characteristics which are different from its rural counterpart. Urban areas have a much higher population density than the rural areas. A substantial proportion of urban population earns its bread and butter from sources other than agriculture. The urban society is basically a consumer society and, therefore, the service sector is an important component of the urban economy.

The recent spurt in the process of urbanisation in the developing countries has attracted the demographers, sociologists, economists, development planners, etc. to study the causes and consequences of urbanisation. According to the estimates prepared by United Nations, about 45 per cent of World population in 1995 was living in urban areas. This proportion is expected to increase to more than 60 per cent by the year 2030. In the less developed countries of the World, the urban population is expected to increase from 34.7 per cent in 1995 to 57.3 per cent in 2030 (United Nations, 1998).

The pattern of urbanisation in the developing countries that we are witnessing today from that witnessed in the developed countries in the past. Urbanisation in the developing countries is characterised by a heavy concentration of population in one or two cities resulting in the phenomenon of primacy and culminating in unsatisfactory spatial distribution of population. Such an urban population growth has created a lot of imbalances within the large cities themselves and has become a major development challenge in the context of improvements in the quality of life.

Urbanisation in India

India has a long and rich history of urbanization with many cities serving as religious, ceremonial, military, administrative and market centres till the beginning of the twentieth century.

A major role in the growth of urban centres was played by the Moughals and the British who established new towns and cities for administrative and other convenience. After Independence, the industrialisation and modernisation process and reorganisation of the States led to the emergence of new urban centres.

Information on levels of urbanisation, its trends and patterns in India is available basically from the population census which is being carried out at every 10 years without any interruption since 1881. The definition of urban areas in different censuses in India, however, has not been uniform. In the population censuses during the British rule, characterisation of an area as urban was basically the responsibility of the Census Superintendent though some broad outlines were laid down to define an area as an Urban area. The concept of the urban area was accorded an objective definition at the time of 1971 population census only. In the 1981 and 1991 population censuses, there has been little change in the definition of the urban area.

During the 1991 population census, the following definition was adopted to classify an area as urban:

> "A human settlement is defined as 'Urban' if it fulfills any one of the following criteria
>
> 1   All places with a municipality, corporation, cantonment board or notified town area committee, etc.

2   All other places which satisfy the following criteria

    i   a minimum population of 5000;

    ii   at least 75 per cent of male working population engaged in non-agriculture pursuits

    iii   a population density of at least 400 km^2.

Besides, the Directors of Census Operations in every State/Union Territories were also allowed to include some places having some distinct characteristics as urban even if such places did not strictly satisfy all the criteria given above in consultation with the concerned State Government/Union Territory Administration and the Census Commissioner of India, (Government of India, 1991). Moreover, the outgrowths of cities and towns have also been treated as urban in the population census.

According to the above definition, two distinct types of urban units have been identified in the population census:

1.   The places which have been classified as urban by virtue of statutory notifications and so statutory towns.

2.   Places which satisfy the criterion 2 of the definition of an urban area as defined above and are referred to as census towns.

A detailed description of various urbanisation concepts adopted during the 1991 census is given elsewhere (Government of India, 1984). An important concept used in the 1991 population census is that of urban agglomeration. An urban agglomerate is a continuous spread and normally consists of a town and its adjoining urban outgrowths, or two or more physically contiguous towns together with contiguous, well-recognised outgrowths, if any, of such towns. This concept of urban agglomerate is a refined version of the concept of 'Town Group' adopted for the first time in the 1961 population census. Essentially, the urban agglomerate gives a broad picture of urban spread.

Number of Towns

At the time of 1901 population census, there were 1888 towns of different population size in the country. By the 1991 population census, this number increased to 4689 meaning that over a period of 90 years, 2801 villages were classified as towns because of the increase in their population. Out of these 4689 towns, 2996 were statutory towns and 1693 were census or non-municipal towns.

In the Indian census, the concept of urban agglomeration is used to join two or more physically contiguous towns with contiguous well-recognised outgrowths, if any, of such towns. As the result, a number of towns identified according to the definition of a town are merged in an urban agglomeration. Thus total number of actual urban agglomerations and isolated towns in the country are actually less than the total number of towns identified and counted in the 1991 census according to the definition adopted by the Census Commissioner. As such, total number of urban agglomerations and towns in the country in 1901 were 1827 which increased to 3768 in the year 1991. In other words, over a period of 90 years, the number of urban agglomerations and isolated towns in the country has nearly doubled.

The census convention is to classify urban agglomerations and isolated towns into six categories according to their population size. These are:

Class I	100000 and more
Class II	50000 - 99999
Class III	20000 - 49999
Class IV	10000 - 19999
Class V	5000 - 9999
Class VI	Below 5000.

The distribution of the towns according to the above size class is given in table 1. A very rapid increase in the number of Class I towns is clear from the table. In fact, as one moves from Class I to Class VI, the increase in the number of towns decreases and in case of Class V and Class VI, the number of towns have decreased instead of increasing. Within the class I towns, the increase in the number of towns was particularly sharp in the large cities. In 1901, there was only one city having a population of more than a million - Calcutta Urban Agglomeration. Till 1941, the number of million plus cities in the country were only two - Calcutta and Bombay. However, after 1941, the number of million plus cities in the country increased rapidly and by 1991, there were 23 million plus cities in the country.

The above shift in the proportionate structure of different size class of towns in the country clearly reflects the rapid increase in the urban population largely due to migration from rural to urban areas. In 1901, the average size of an urban dwelling unit was just around 14 thousand which increased to nearly 58 thousand by the year 1991. Clearly, not only the number of urban agglomeration and isolated towns have increased but there has also been some significant expansion of the existing urban agglomerations and towns during the last 90 years.

Levels and Trends in Urban Population
At the beginning of this century, total urban population of the country was about 25.85 million or nearly 11 per cent of the total population of the country. By the year 1991, the urban population of the country increased to more than 217 million which accounts for more than one fourth of the total population of the country. This means that over a period of 90 years, the urban population of the country has increased by almost eight times.

Information about the trends in urbanization in the country is given in table 2. With time, the decennial rate of growth has also increased. The only exceptions are a sudden increase in the growth rate during the decade 1941-51; a rapid decrease during the decade 1951-61 and a slow down in the decennial growth rate during the decade 1981-91. This rapid increase in the decennial growth rate during 1941-51 is generally attributed to large influx of refugees in the country as the result of partition at the time of Independence. These refugees did not spread in rural areas but settled in towns. On the other hand, Bose had attributed the slump in decennial growth rate during 1951-61 to definitional changes at the time of 1961 (Bose, 1977). Finally, reasons for a decrease in the decennial growth rate of urban population during the decade 1981-91 are not known at present. There is however little indication of any urban turnaround.

Of particular interest, however, is the changing size class distribution of urban population over time. The increasing dominance of class I cities in the urban hierarchy is very well reflected by the information collected in table 3. In 1901, class I cities, cities having a population of 0.1 million and more, accounted for about 23 per cent of the total urban population of the country. By the year 1991, this proportion increased to almost 65 per cent indicating an increase in the concentration of the urban population in class I towns. At the same time, while there has been very little decrease in the proportion of urban population in class II and class III towns, the proportion of urban population in class IV, class V and class VI towns has decreased sharply. For example, in 1901, population in class V towns accounted for more than one fifth of the total urban population of the country. This proportion, in 1991, reduced to just 2.6 per cent. Similarly, the proportion of urban population living in class IV towns reduced from 22.1 per cent in 1901 to 7.9 per in 1991 and the proportion of urban population living in class VI towns from 6.3 per cent in 1901 to only 0.3 per cent in 1991. This trend in the process of urbanization in the country is due to both, increase in the size of average urban spatial unit as well as preference for migration to class I and class II cities in comparison to class IV, class V and class VI towns. In fact, nearly all migration from rural to urban areas in the country is confined to class I, class II and class III towns. Migration from rural to class IV, class V and class VI towns is very marginal. The reason is that most of these towns are not growth centres.

Within the class I towns themselves, growth of million plus cities need special reference here as they have recorded an unprecedented growth and expansion in recent years. In 1901, there was only one million plus city in the country namely Calcutta Urban Agglomeration. This number increased to 2 in 1911 and remained unchanged till 1951 when the number of million plus cities in the country increased to 5. After 1951, there has literally been an explosion of million plus cities in the country and by 1991, the number of cities having a population of more than a million increased to 23. In between 1981 and 1991 alone, the number of million plus cities in the country increased by 11.

Along with the increase in the number of million plus cities in the country, the proportion of population accounted by these cities has also increased substantially with the result that there is now a very heavy concentration of urban population in these cities. In 1901, the population of the only million plus city in the country accounted for less than 6 per cent of the total urban population. By the year 1991, nearly one third of the total urban population of the country was living in million plus cities. At the same time, the average size of the million plus cities has also increased from about 1.51 million in 1901 to more than 3 million in 1991. It appears that the urban population is increasingly and rapidly concentrating in the large cities of the country.

Information on the degree or the extent of urbanization can be judged from the urban/rural population ratio and the town size class in which the median urban inhabitant is located. In 1901, there were 1216 inhabitants in the urban areas for every 10000 inhabitants in the rural areas. By 1991, this proportion increased to 3463 urban inhabitants for every 10000 rural inhabitants. In other words, the number of urban inhabitants for every rural inhabitant has increased by almost three times during the last 90 years.

The extent of urbanization can also be judged from the town size class in which the median urban inhabitant is residing. It may be seen from table 5 that up to the year 1941, the urban median inhabitant was residing in the town size class III, i.e. a town with a population ranging between a 20000to 49999. However, since 1961, the median urban inhabitant is residing in the town size class I.

Similarly, a rapid growth of urbanization in the country is clear from the trend in average annual exponential growth rate in the urban population. As may be seen from table 5, the average annual rate of growth of urban population in the country has also increased over time. During the decade 1901-11, the growth of urban population in the country was almost stationary; the urban population increased at the rate of just 0.03 per cent per year only. By contrast, during the decade 1971-81, the rate of urban population growth in the country reached an all time high of 3.79 per cent per year. During the decade 1981-91, the urban population growth rate has however, decrease slightly indicating some slow down in the urban population growth.

Tempo of Urbanization
Unlike the degree and the growth of urbanisation which have shown , more or less, increasing trend throughout the century, the tempo of urbanisation in the country has followed a

fluctuating trend as is clear from table 6. The tempo of urbanization in the country was at its peak during the decade 1941-51 mainly because of a very large influx of refugees in the country as the result of partition and subsequent migration. The tempo of urbanization has also been found to be very high during the decade 1971-81 largely due to the classification of a large number of rural areas as urban areas. However, in comparison to the decade 1971-81, the tempo of urbanization appears to have slowed down during the decade 1981-91. This indicates that in the years to come, the process of urbanization in the country is expected to slow down.

Concentration of Urban Population

Both the degree and growth as well as the tempo of urbanization, however, reveal only one direction of the urbanization process - the level of urbanisation. They do not show how urban population is distributed over urban units of different sizes. Two populations having same degree of urbanisation may have entirely different size structure and so there is a need to measure the size structure of urban population. The measures used, generally, are scale of urbanisation, Gini's index, concentration index, ran-size rule, etc.

In table 7, estimates of three measures of urban concentration are presented. All three measure clearly indicate increasing concentration of urban population in Class I towns. This means that the distribution of the urban population over different size class of towns is getting more and more skewed. This indicates that in addition to migration from rural to urban areas, some very significant migration within the urban population - from smaller towns to larger towns and cities has also taken place in the country.

Some of the measures of different aspects of urbanisation for different States of the country are presented in table 8. These measures show wide variation across the States. Interestingly, the number of urban units have decreased in a number of States in 1991 as compared to 1951 whereas in other States, the number of urban units have increased sharply. There are two reasons for the decrease in the number of towns. First is the declassification of the town because it does not fit into the definition of an urban area as defined in the census. For example, in the 1991 census, 93 locations classified as urban in the 1981 census were declassified into villages. The definition of the urban area, it may be pointed out, has been changed at almost all censuses.

Another reason behind the decrease in the number of urban units in the country is the introduction of the concept of 'urban agglomerations' in the 1991 census. As the result of the introduction of this concept, 103 of small towns were merged with the adjoining larger towns and cities in the 1991 census. However, this reclassification has not affected the total urban population of the country.

The index of the growth of urban population also varies widely across the Sates. The index of growth of Class I towns has been found to be significantly higher than the index of growth of urban population in some States and almost same in other States. In Uttar Pradesh and West Bengal, for example, there is not much different between the index of the growth of urban population and index of the growth of Class I cities. In other States, however, the situation is different.

In general, urban population has increased five to seven times in most of the States. Urban population increase has been relatively slower in Uttar Pradesh, West Bengal, Tamilnadu, Punjab and Maharashtra. On the other hand, in Orissa, urban population increased by more than 18 times between 1951 and 1991.

The degree of urbanization, measured by the proportion of population urban and urban-rural ratio has been found to be highest in Maharashtra followed by Gujrat and Tamilnadu. In all the three States, the urban population constituted more than half of the rural population of the State at the time of 1991 census. In both Maharashtra and Gujrat, rapid urbanization appears to be the result of rapid urbanization that has taken place in this States after Independence. By contrast, in Himachal Pradesh, urban population, in 1991, was less than 10 per cent of the rural population of the State. In Bihar, Orissa and Uttar Pradesh, urban population in 1991 was less than one fourth of the rural population.

The concentration of urban population in Class I cities is also clear from table 9. Barring Himachal Pradesh and Orissa, in all the States of the country included in the table, more than 50 per cent of the total urban population was residing in the Class I towns at the time of 1991 census. This proportion was found to be highest in West Bengal where four of every five urban inhabitants were living in Class I towns. In Maharashtra, on the other hand, this proportion was found to be more than 77 per cent. The concentration of urban population in Class I towns is also reflected in the Gini's index of concentration which has been found to be highest in Maharashtra and second highest in West Bengal.

Gujrat and Tamilnadu are two States where a relatively less concentration of population in Class I cities has been observed despite the fact that the degree of urbanization in these States is amongst the highest in the country. On the other hand, the high degree of urbanization in Maharashtra is associated with a high concentration of urban population in Class I towns. Obviously, the pattern of urbanization in Gujrat and Tamilnadu is basically different from that in Maharashtra and West Bengal.

As regards the tempo of urbanisation, Kerala singles out amongst the States included in table 9. During the decade 1981-91, the tempo of urbanization in Kerala has been found to be exceptionally high because of both, a very rapid growth of urban population and a very slow growth of rural population. It appears that both, migration from rural to urban areas and classification of villages as towns due to increase in population are responsible for a very high tempo of urbanization in the State. Other States where tempo of urbanization has been found to be high in comparison to other States are Andhra Pradesh and Madhya Pradesh. By contrast, tempo of urbanization has been found to be extremely low in West Bengal, Tamilnadu and Bihar.

The above review of pattern of urbanization in different States of the country suggest that every State has its own pattern of urbanization and there are few similarities. In Maharashtra and West Bengal, for example, there is very high concentration of urban population in large cities, particularly the primate cities. By contrast in Gujrat and Tamilnadu, the degree of urbanization is very high but the urban population is fairly scattered, not concentrated in a few large cities. Finally, the tempo of urbanization is not high in these States but in Kerala where the population is already at an advanced stage of demographic transition.

City Population Growth

We have seen in the previous section that the growth of population in large cities has been very substantial, particularly, after 1951. According to 1991 census, there were 300 cities with more than 0.1 million population. These cities contained a population of 138.8 million out of the total urban population of 212.8 million. Thus, in 1991, more than 65 per cent of the urban population was residing in towns with a population of 0.1 million and more. Moreover, the average annual population growth rate of the Class I towns has been faster than the growth rate of other towns. During the 40 years between 1951 through 1991, the population of Class I towns increased at a rate of 4.05 per cent year on average. By contrast, the population of Class II towns increased at an average annual growth rate of 3.34 per cent per year only.

Among the Class I towns, there is a very heavy concentration of population in the million plus cities. At the time of 1991 population census, the 23 million plus cities in the country, alone, accounted for more than half of the total population of Class I towns. In fact, the Gini's index of population concentration in the Class I towns has been found to be 0.580 which confirms a high degree of concentration of population in million plus cities.

Among the 23 million plus cities in the country, the distribution of the population has again been found to be highly skewed. There were 14 cities with a population of 1-2 million. These 14 cities accounted for only about 8 per cent of the total population in the million plus cities. By contrast, there were just 4 cities with a population of more than 5 million. These 4 cities accounted for 17 per cent of the total population in million plus cities. Clearly, within the million plus cities also, the distribution of the population is skewed.

During the forty years between 1951and 1991, the population of cities in the country increased at an average annual rate of growth of 4.05 per cent per year. By comparison, the average annual population growth rate in the million plus cities was less, 3.33 per cent per year whereas, in million minus cities, population increased at an average annual growth rate of 5.11 per cent per year. However, despite a relatively slower growth, the addition to the population of million plus cities in absolute numbers continue to be very substantial. In the forty years since 1951, nearly 52 million population has been added to the 23 cities classified as million plus in 1991.

Among the million plus cities, according to the 1991 census, Greater Bombay was the largest city in the country with a population of 12.57 million followed by Calcutta (10.92 million, Delhi (8.38 million) and Madras (5.36 million).

The most rapid population growth among the million plus cities has been recorded in Bhopal in Madhya Pradesh where the population increased at an average annual growth rate of 5.85 per cent per year during the decade 1981-91. The other million plus city which has recorded an average annual growth rate of more than 5 per cent during the last forty years is Vishakhapatnam. By contrast, in five cities, average annual population growth rate has been found to be less than 3 per cent per year. The slowest average annual population growth rate has, however, been recorded in Calcutta during the period under reference.

Primacy
Primacy is an important consequence of urbanisation. Primacy means concentration of large urban population in one or two primate cities. In India, the primate city phenomenon does not exist, at least in the national context as values of almost all types of primacy indexes are not very high. The reason is simple. It has growth centres scattered all over the country because of regional and cultural diversity. Before the British rule, the country was divided into numerous princely States each having its own capital as a big or small growth centre. Even during the British rule many of these centres flourished. The British, at the same time, developed their own growth centres for their administrative convenience. After the Independence, the reorganisation of States resulted in a number of new growth centres in the from of State capitals. Moreover, a completely new class of industrial townships come up as a result of industrialisation since Independence.

The four city primacy index in India in the year 1991 has been estimated to be only 0.51 while the eleven city primacy index has been estimated to be 0.57. This shows that as far as India is concerned, the process of urbanisation has not resulted in the emergence of one or two primate cities as it has happened in many developing countries. However, both the primacy indexes have shown an increasing trend over the year. The four city and eleven city primacy index in 1951 were 0.39 and 0.47 per cent respectively.

At the State level, the four city primacy index varies widely. Highest primacy index has been observed in West Bengal where the population of the primate city, Calcutta, is nearly 7.5 times more than the total population of the next three most populous cities. In most of the smaller States also, the primacy index has been found to be well above 1, indicating a concentration of urban population in the primate cities.

It appears that the phenomenon of primacy is closely linked with the size of the population. In smaller State the State capital has emerged as the prominent primate city. The administrative nuclearisation and associated trade activities appear to be a major reason behind the eruption of primate cities. This observation is supported by the analysis at the district level. In most of the districts of the country in all the States, a very substantial proportion of urban population is concentrated in district headquarter towns.

An interesting feature of primacy in India is that it is primarily confined to east and northeast region of the country. In other parts of the country the urban population is well scattered and there is no concentration of population in primate cities. This is particularly so in the large States of the country with the only exception of Maharashtra.

Urban Pattern

Nehru, in his autobiography, has characterised a city of British India as one which is polarized between "Anglostan and Hindustan". The Hindustan of the city was the densely crowded city proper which provided most of the resources for managing the city but which received very little out of these resources. On the other hand, the Anglostan was a widespread area of bungalows, gardens and lawns where British officials lived along with Indian elite. This part of the city popularly known as the "Civil lines" provided very little resources for the management and maintenance of the city but used most of the available resources (Nehru, 1962).

The situation remains more or less same even today - in Independent India - thanks to the legacy of the British rule. The core of the city remains neglected, while its poorer parts are almost ignored. By contrast, the "civil lines" type localities continue to flourish with more and more Indian elite settling there. In the large cities, there are serious problems of irrational land utilisation, inefficient development, large scale physical deterioration, acute housing shortages and above all, environmental degradation. On the other hand, in smaller urban centres there are problems of impoverishment, and lack of even minimum infrastructure and services. Over the years, a new form of dichotomy has developed in which an affluent urban minority flourishes at the cost of a deprived urban majority.

The magnification of problems arising out of an imbalanced urban structure may be seen at its maximum at the metropolitan level. Here, these problems are compounded further by the lack of a dispersed pattern of work-centres, sprawling dormitories and suburbs creating transport problems, and proliferation of slums and squatter settlements which, practically, have no basic amenities and services infrastructure. Skyrocketing land and property values in these cities have resulted grabbing of vacant land. But despite all these problems, these cities continue to attract both monetary and human capital, resulting in further aggravation of problems, which already have serious dimensions. Unfortunately, no attempt has so far been made to fully evaluate the social cost of these large city concentrations.

Consequences of Urbanisation: The case of Greater Bombay

Urbanisation, at least in the theoretical sense, is seen as a process by which the surplus working population in rural areas can resettle in economic and social growth centres where non-agriculture job opportunities are available. As such, urbanisation can be a catalyst for economic growth and development if opportunities in urban areas are productive and lead to gainful employment. On the other hand, if urbanisation is merely a process of transfer of rural poverty, it only results in a concentration of misery and deterioration of urban environment.

In India the urbanisation process has basically been a continuation of the phenomenon started during the British rule - concentration of focus on major cities and near ignorance of rural agriculture sector. The British followed this form of urbanisation for their convenience. But it resulted in a phenomenal increase in rural-urban socioeconomic disparities. In the early years of Independence, the process continued as the development planners opted for industrialisation for rapid economic progress and nearly ignored rural agriculture sector. It was only after 1975, that the government started paying any serious attention for the development for rural agriculture sector.

As a result, the urban centres, particularly the metropolitan cities continued to grow rapidly by attracting large number of migrants not only from the rural areas but also from small unproductive areas as well. Even today, these metropolitan cities provide better employment opportunities to all category of workers and, therefore, continue to pull migrants into themselves. But this influx of migrants combined with the natural increase of the cities led to a substantial growth in their size making them almost unmanageable.

Greater Bombay may be cited as the example of a city which is in deep crisis but continues to attract people both educated and uneducated from all parts of the country. The case of Greater Bombay is an interesting one as it provides a deeper insight into the issues related to the uncontrolled urbanisation process that is taking place in all developing countries.

Greater Bombay, popularly known as the commercial capital of India grew from a population of just 10 thousand in 1661 to 12.57 million in 1991, making it 6th largest city of the World. The core of Greater Bombay lies in the long narrow island which is commonly known as Island city or Bombay city. In

1991, 9.91 million people were residing in this tiny island which accounts for nearly 75 per cent of the population of Greater Bombay. According to United Nations estimates, the population of the city is expected to reach 18.0 million by 2000 AD (United Nations, 1998).

Before its occupation by the East India Company, Bombay was basically a fishermen's town. Growth of Bombay as a city can be traced in the increasing hold of the British in India. Its natural harbour, and its closeness to both the rich hinterland of Gangatic planes and the western countries has made it the most important port town of the country. The opening of Suez Canal after Second World War gave another boost to the growth of the city. The partition of the country at the time of Independence, brought in a large chunk of refuges. In between 1941 and 1951, alone, the population of the city increased by 1.158 million at an average annual growth rate of 5.2 per cent per year, highest ever recorded since 1900. Since, 1951 though the average annual rate of growth of population has shown a somewhat declining trend yet the net addition to the city's existing population has increased in every decade. Between 1981 and 1991, alone, more than 4.33 million people were added to city's population.

Most of the growth in the population of the city has been absorbed in suburban areas. In the core city of Greater Bombay, the Island city, population increase during 1981-91, population increase was only about 20 per cent compared to more than 33 per cent for the whole city. Apparently, the core city has reached its limits and there appears to be no scope even to accommodate the natural increase of its own population.

Both migration as well as natural increase have contributed almost equally to population growth in the city in recent years. Between 1971-81, nearly 47.8 per cent of the increase in population was due to the natural increase of its population itself while remaining was due to migration. But the continuing migration of unskilled workers to Bombay has become a highly political and socially sensitive issue.

In any case, the enormous increase in population of the city has put considerable pressure on its management which at times seems crumbling. There is a serious housing problem with two of every five persons in the city living in slums, according to a survey conducted in 1976. Another survey has revealed that a substantial proportion of city's population lives in some 20,000 tenements (chawls), 84 per cent of which were constructed before 1940 and which are very poorly maintained because of rent control (Maharashtra Housing and Area Development Authority, 1982).

The same is true for water supply. Because of the big gap in demand and supply, water supply is restricted to only two to six hours per day depending upon the location. The core city of the Bombay has access to sewage system but it is inadequate and outdated. About 45 per cent of houses of the city have no water and sewage facility. The city suffers from serious air pollution mainly from noxious industries rather than from automobile emissions. Interestingly, Bombay does not exhibit a typical set of transportation problems as found in other mega-cities. Public transport accounts for 90 per cent of all person trips. Car ownership rates are low and cars have accounted for 40 per cent of road traffic and only 20 per cent of road passengers (Richardson, 1980). But the public transport system is inadequate to meet the demand and because of the geography of the city there is very little scope for future expansion of transport network.

Most of the resources for the management of the city are derived from internal sources as the contributions of Government of India and State government are small (11 and 14 per cent of the total revenue respectively). But the earning from internal sources are not adequate to meet the ever increasing demand which is the result of ever increasing population.

Despite all these problems associated with the city, its economies of scale heavily outweigh its diseconomies. Bombay's economy has been very strong in recent years Its base is oriented towards international and national markets rather than regional markets and it has a vigorous and diversified manufacturing sector. The city handles more than one quarter of country's foreign trade and generates one tenth of nation's industrial jobs, and two elevenths of manufacturing value added. The structure of employment, expectedly, is dominated by secondary and tertiary sectors with little scope for primary sector. The unemployment rate is considerably low (4.8 per cent) suggesting that despite massive growth of population the city has been able to meet the employment needs of the growing population. There is also some evidence that some of the benefits of economic growth have "trickled down" especially since 1975 thus making the city even more attractive to migrants.

Urban Policy

For such a large country like India Having as many as 23 million plus cities, no uniform set of urban policy may suffice. Still major or broad dimensions of the urban policy remain same throughout the country. Here, we first discuss the policy at the national level and then explore it in some detail in the context of urbanisation and its consequences in Greater Bombay.

Any urban policy has two components - policy related to spatial distribution and policy related to the management of urban centres. The focus of attention of the urban policy in India, however, has been on the spatial distribution policy only. It is generally presumed that nearly all the problems of urban management can be traced in the improper spatial distribution of population and its manifestation in many forms of which, primacy, eruption of large cities etc. are a few. An elaboration of spatial distribution policy and the programmes started to implement such a policy, therefore, seems to be more appropriate in the discussion of urbanisation patterns, and issues in India.

There is no formal national policy on urbanisation in India. But successive Five Year Plans had emphasized urbanisation as an important aspect of the process of economic and social development. Recently, the government has adopted strategies that may help in controlling migration to large cities and metropolises. The Sixth Five Year plan states that the thrust of India's urbanisation policy during the next decade will be to give greater emphasis to the provision of adequate infrastructure and other facilities in small towns and intermediate cities that have hitherto been neglected.

A synthesis of the strategies adopted and the instruments being applied to modify the spatial distribution of population and to check migration to cities, particularly, metropolitan cities is given in table 12. The government regards the existing spatial distribution in the country only marginal unsatisfactory and desires only minor changes in the existing pattern. This desire of the government has been explicitly stated in various policy statements. An initiative that merits attention is the appointment, for the first time, a national commission on urbanisation. It was for the first time that a body constituted by experts from various disciplines discussed at length various issues related to the process of urbanisation and suggested some concrete recommendations.

Coming to Greater Bombay, its ills have been the focus of attention right from the days of the Independence. The general consensus in numerous studies and group reports is the excessive spatial concentration in the southern part of Bombay island. Many decentralisation strategies have been proposed to combat the problem at various points of time. The first strategy was the industrial dispersal. In the late 1960s, a group of architects put forward the idea of a new Bombay across the harbour which was endorsed at the government level in the 1970 Bombay Metropolitan Regional Plan. Along with the New Bombay project, the government has also started the development of Bandra-Kurla complex and Kalyan complex that may act as magnets to attract the entrepreneurs from both Bombay as well as from the hinterland. In essence, population redistribution policies have so far been the mainstay of the attempts to tackle the ills of Greater Bombay.

Though, the population redistribution programme has been taken at a large scale to cure the ills of Greater Bombay, very little attention has been paid to check the flow of people into the city by direct interventions. The attempts to check the flow of migrants into the city continue to be indirect ones - development of new towns, rural development etc. It is however not known how far these attempts have been successful. It may be pointed out in this context that the indirect strategies and approaches may be helpful in checking influx into core city or into areas of high concentration, they play little role in checking rural - urban migration. Rather, these programmes and activities have even contributed to accelerate such migration as new growth centres attract more people from rural to urban areas because of the economies of the scale.

Conclusions
Although India has been engaged in farsighted economic planning since Independence, very little attention appears to have been paid in the development planning process in the country to spatial aspects of social and economic change. This lack of spatial concern in the national planning process has resulted in spontaneous patterns of urbanisation. For example, at the national level, the primacy in urban spatial structure may not be significantly dominant but at the regional level, the concentration of population in primate cities is apparent. Attempts in infusing a spatial concern in the planning process are definitely inadequate.

A major push in this direction may be the development and implementation of Regional Development plans. In the context of metropolitan cities, such a plan becomes all the more relevant as in Greater Bombay, most of the migrants are from poor and arid district of Ratnagiri. Just relocating the population is not the answer to the problems of a city where more than half of the growth is due to migration.

Controlling migration requires, basically, focus on push factors rather than pull factors. Because of an economic system that gives greater weight to capital investment than to the human investment, urban areas will continue to pull rural masses. But if the rural areas are developed properly, the migration will be a productive one - a migration that will contribute to the economic development of the city, region and the country. It will not be the transfer of rural poverty into urban areas, as is the case today.

References

Bose, A (1977) Urbanisation in India: A Demographic perspective. In S. Goldstein and D.F. Sly (eds.) *Patterns of Urbanisation: comparative country studies*. Ordina Editions.

Government of India (1981) *Census Paper No. 2 of 1981*. New Delhi, Registrar general.

Government of India (1984) *Urban Growth in India 1951-81*. Census Monograph No. 1. New Delhi, Registrar General.

Government of India (1988) *Report of the National commission on Urbanisation*. New Delhi, Deptt. of Urban Affairs.

Government of Maharashtra (1982) *Affordable low Income Shelter programme in Bombay Metropolitan Region*. Bombay, BMRDA and Maharashtra Housing and Area Development Authority.

National Institute of Urban Affairs (1988) *State of India's Urbanisation*. New Delhi, National Institute of Urban Affairs.

Nehru, JL (1962) *An Autobiography*. New Delhi, Jawaharlal Nehru Memorial Trust.

United Nations (1962) *World Population Prospects, 1988*. New York, United Nations.

United Nations (1982) *Population of India*. Bangkok, Economic and Social Commission for Asia and Pacific.

United Nations (1998) *World Urbanization Prospects: 1996 Revision*. New York, United Nations.

Table 1: Number of towns in the country by size class.

	Year	1901	1911	1921	1931	1941	1951	1961	1971	1981	1991
Town class											
I	Number	24	23	29	35	49	76	102	148	216	296
	Index	100	96	121	146	204	317	425	617	900	1233
II	Number	43	40	45	56	74	91	129	173	270	341
	Index	100	93	105	130	172	212	300	402	628	793
III	Number	130	135	145	183	242	327	437	558	738	927
	Index	100	104	112	141	186	252	336	429	568	713
IV	Number	391	364	370	434	498	608	719	827	1053	1135
	Index	100	93	95	111	127	155	184	212	269	290
V	Number	744	707	734	800	920	1124	711	623	739	725
	Index	100	95	99	108	124	151	96	84	99	97
VI	Number	479	485	571	509	407	569	172	147	229	185
	Index	100	101	119	106	85	119	36	31	48	39
All	Number	1811	1754	1894	2017	2190	2795	2270	2476	3245	3609
	Index	100	97	105	111	121	154	125	137	179	199

Remarks

1. Excludes Assam and Jammu and Kashmir

2. All classes exclude six towns in 1941, four each in 1931 and 1921 and 2 each in 1911 and 1901 of Goa which could not be assigned to any size class as their population for these years are not available.

264

Table 2:   Trends in Urbanization in India

Year	Number of UAs/ Towns	Total population (Million)	Urban population		
			Total (Million)	Proportion of total population (per cent)	Decennial growth rate (per cent)
1901	1827	238.40	25.85	10.84	
1911	1815	252.09	25.94	10.29	0.35
1921	1949	251.32	28.09	11.18	8.27
1931	2072	278.98	33.46	11.99	19.12
1941	2250	318.66	44.15	13.86	31.97
1951	2843	361.09	62.44	17.29	41.42
1961	2365	439.23	78.94	17.97	26.41
1971	2590	548.16	109.11	19.91	38.23
1981	3378	683.33	159.46	23.34	46.14
1991	3768	844.32	217.18	25.72	36.19

Remarks: Includes interpolated figures for Assam for 1981 and projected figures for Jammu and Kashmir for 1991 as census could not be carried out in Assam in 1981 and in Jammu and Kashmir in 1991.

Table 3:   Size Class Distribution of Urban Population

Year	I	II	III	IV	V	VI
1901	22.90	11.80	16.50	22.10	20.40	6.30
1911	24.20	10.90	17.50	20.50	19.80	6.90
1921	25.30	12.50	16.90	18.90	19.00	7.40
1931	27.40	11.90	18.80	19.00	17.30	5.60
1941	35.40	11.80	17.70	16.30	15.40	3.40
1951	41.80	11.10	16.70	14.00	13.20	3.20
1961	48.40	11.90	18.50	13.00	7.20	1.00
1971	55.80	11.30	16.30	11.30	4.70	0.60
1981	60.40	11.70	14.30	9.50	3.60	0.50
1991	64.90	11.00	13.30	7.90	2.60	0.30

Table 4:   Growth of Million Plus Cities.

Year	Number of million plus cities	Total population (Million)	Average population per city (million)	Proportion to total urban population (per cent)	Average annual growth rate
1901	1	1.51	1.51	5.84	
1911	2	2.76	1.38	10.65	6.04
1921	2	3.13	1.56	11.14	1.24
1931	2	3.41	1.70	10.18	0.85
1941	2	5.31	2.65	12.02	4.43
1951	5	11.75	2.35	18.81	7.94
1961	7	18.10	2.59	22.93	4.32
1971	9	27.83	3.09	25.51	4.30
1981	12	42.12	3.51	26.41	4.14
1991	23	70.66	3.07	32.54	5.17

Table 5: Degree and growth of urbanization.

Year	Proportion of total population (per cent)	Urban/Rural ratio (per cent)	Town size class in which median urban inhabitant resides	Average annual growth rate (per cent)
1901	10.84	12.16	III	
1911	10.29	11.47	III	0.03
1921	11.18	12.58	III	0.79
1931	11.99	13.63	III	1.75
1941	13.86	16.08	III	2.77
1951	17.29	20.91	II	3.47
1961	17.97	21.91	I	2.34
1971	19.91	24.85	I	3.24
1981	23.34	30.44	I	3.79
1991	25.72	34.63	I	3.09

Table 6:   Tempo of Urbanization.

Year	Urban-rural growth difference (Per cent)	Annual gain in per cent urban	Annual rate of gain in per cent urban (Per cent)
1901			
1911	-0.59	-0.06	-0.52
1921	0.92	0.09	0.82
1931	0.80	0.08	0.71
1941	1.66	0.19	1.44
1951	2.62	0.34	2.22
1961	0.47	0.07	0.38
1971	1.26	0.19	1.02
1981	2.03	0.34	1.59
1991	1.29	0.24	0.97

Table 7: Indices of Concentration of Urban Population.

Year	Gini's index	Concentration index	Scale of urbanization
1901	0.558	0.421	6.06
1911	.0567	0.431	5.83
1921	.0579	0.445	6.47
1931	.0590	0.461	7.08
1941	.0618	0.493	8.57
1951	0.654	0.526	11.31
1961	0.657	0.525	11.82
1971	0.672	0.552	13.38
1981	0.688	0.571	16.06
1991	0.696	0.581	17.91

Table 8. State Level Variation in Patterns of Urbanisation.

State	Towns	LC	CLASS I	GUU	GCL1
Andhra Pradesh	213	2	32	77	533
Bihar	211	1	17	209	340
Gujrat	225	3	21	97	350
Haryana	90	0	12	161	-
Himachal Pradesh	55	0	1	190	-
Karnataka	254	1	21	90	350
Kerala	109	1	14	122	350
Madhya Pradesh	433	2	23	223	460
Maharashtra	290	3	27	82	300
Orissa	119	0	7	305	700
Punjab	120	1	10	109	333
Rajasthan	215	1	14	97	350
Tamilnadu	260	3	25	99	313
Uttar Pradesh	702	3	42	153	263
West Bengal	160	1	23	205	1150

Remark : LC = Number of million plus cities in 1991.
CLASSI = Number of Class I towns
GUU = Index of growth of urban units 1951-91 (Base = 1951)
GCL = Growth of Class I towns

Table 9:   State Level Variation in Pattern of
                Urbanization

State	GUP	GPCL	PCL1	URR	PC	GINI Index	URGD
Andhra Pradesh	329	675	66.88	36.70	26.84	0.601	1.879
Bihar	433	665	52.62	15.16	13.17	0.603	0.624
Gujrat	320	553	66.43	52.44	34.40	0.693	1.498
Haryana	418	-	58.54	32.96	24.79	0.596	1.628
Himachal Pradesh	289	-	24.70	9.53	8.70	0.550	1.455
Karnataka	311	552	64.60	44.74	30.91	0.680	0.964
Kerala	420	773	66.34	35.94	26.44	0.611	4.435
Madhya Pradesh	490	742	50.39	30.22	23.21	0.629	1.717
Maharashtra	331	474	77.85	63.20	38.73	0.755	1.588
Orissa	712	1834	44.43	15.52	13.43	0.574	1.487
Punjab	302	495	54.36	42.29	29.72	0.630	0.996
Rajasthan	340	619	50.09	29.67	22.88	0.584	1.071
Tamilnadu	259	410	65.96	51.97	34.20	0.683	0.558
Uttar Pradesh	321	393	55.99	24.83	19.89	0.666	1.266
West Bengal	297	317	81.70	37.73	27.39	0.736	0.469

Remarks :
GUP   =   Index of growth of urban population (1951=100)
GPCL   =   Index of Growth of population in Class I towns.
PCLI   =   per cent of total Urban population in Class I towns in 1991.
URR   =   Urban rural population ratio. in 1991.
PC   =   Proportion of Urban population to total population.
GINI INDEX =   An index of concentration developed by Gini.
URGD   =   Urban Rural growth difference.

Table 10:   Size Class Distribution of Cities (Class I towns)

Class	Number of cities	Population (Million)	Per cent of Population of Class I towns	Per cent of total Urban Population
M1: Less than 200,000	167	22.94	16.42	10.78
M2: 200,000-299,999	40	9.61	6.88	4.51
M3: 300,000-499,999	40	15.59	11.15	7.32
M4: 500,000-999,999	30	20.94	14.98	9.84
M5: 1,000,000 & above	23	70.66	50.57	33.19
Total	300	139.73	100.00	65.64

Population and Development: The Indian Perspective

Table 11:   Million Plus Cities in India, 1991

Class	Number of cities	Population (Million)	Per cent of Population of Class I towns	Per cent of Urban Population
MP1: 1000000-1999999	14	17.18	24.31	8.07
MP2: 2000000-4999999	5	16.26	23.01	7.64
MP3: 5000000 & above	4	37.22	52.68	17.49
Total	23	70.66	100.00	33.19

Table 12:   Growth of Million Plus Cities in India.

Name of the city	State	Population		Growth rate
		1951	1991	
Bombay	Maharashtra	2966902	12571720	3.61
Calcutta	W Bengal	4669559	10916272	2.12
Delhi	Delhi	1437134	8375188	4.41
Madras	Tamilnadu	1542333	5361468	3.11
Hyderabad	Andhra Pradesh	1130688	4280261	3.33
Banglore	Karnataka	786343	4086548	4.12
Ahmedabad	Gujrat	877329	3297655	3.31
Pune	Maharashtra	608634	2485014	3.52
Kanpur	Uttar Pradesh	705383	2111284	2.74
Nagpur	Maharashtra	485264	1661409	3.08
Lucknow	Uttar Pradesh	496861	1642134	2.99
Surat	Gujrat	237394	1517076	4.64
Jaipur	Rajasthan	30438	1514425	4.01
Kochi	Kerala	177134	1139543	4.65
Coimbtore	Tamilnadu	287334	1135549	3.44
Vadodra	Ahmedabad	211407	1115265	4.16
Indore	Madhya Pradesh	310959	1104065	3.17
Patna	Bihar	326163	1098572	3.04
Madurai	Tamilnadu	370791	1093572	2.70
Bhopal	Madhya Pradesh	102333	1063662	5.85
Vishakha patnam	Andhra Pradesh	108042	1051918	5.69
Varanasi	Uttar Pradesh	369799	1026467	2.55
Ludhiana	Punjab	153795	1012062	4.71
Total		18665961	70661129	3.33

Table 13:   Primacy Index at State level.

State	Primate city	Category	Primacy index	Proportion of urban population
Andhra Pradesh	Hyderabad	Capital	1.807	24.03
Bihar	Patna	Capital	0.485	9.66
Goa	Mormugao	Commercial	0.483	19.04
Gujrat	Ahmedabad	Capital	1.004	23.28
Haryana	Faridabad	Commercial	0.980	15.17
Himachal Pradesh	Shimla	Capital	1.644	24.70
Karnataka	Banglore	Capital	2.368	29.50
Kerala	Kochi	Commercial	0.545	14.84
Madhya Pradesh	Indore	Commercial	0.413	7.19
Maharashtra	Bombay	Capital	2.582	41.22
Manipur	Imphal	Capital	2.208	39.66
Meghalaya	Shilong	Capital	2.752	67.54
Mizoram	Aizwal	Capital	2.203	48.68
Nagaland	Dimapur	Capital	0.577	27.09
Orissa	Cuttack	Commercial	0.430	10.38
Punjab	Ludhiana	Commercial	0.676	16.87
Rajasthan	Jaipur	Capital	0.946	15.08
Sikkim	Gangtok	Capital	2.834	67.52
Tamilnadu	Madras	Capital	1.823	28.18
Tripura	Agartala	Capital	1.757	37.62
Uttar Pradesh	Kanpur	Commercial	0.583	7.63
West Bengal	Calcutta	Capital	7.479	58.62

Table 14: Strategies and Instruments Adopted for
Influencing Spatial Distribution

Strategies	Instruments
• Slowing of metropolitan growth • Promotions of small towns and intermediate cities • Counter magnets • New tows • Regional development policies for lagging regions • Rural development strategies	• Public infrastructure subsidies and/or development • Grants, loans and tax incentives to new industries and relocatees. • Direct State investment • Direct restrictions and controls on industrial locations. • Transport rate and other interregional costs adjustments • Housing and social services • Human resources investment and job training.

Printed in the United States
127461LV00002B/21/A